GW00854599

SME GLOBALISATION

How to Maximize Your Company Value in a Cost Efficient Way

Sandy Damm

10-10-10 Publishing

Best wishes

Sandy

SME GLOBALISATION: How to Maximize Your Company Value in a Cost Efficient Way
www.smeglobalisation.com
Copyright © 2021 Sandy Damm

ISBN: 979-8-733453-30-9

Publisher
10-10-10 Publishing
Markham, ON Canada

Printed in United Kingdom

TABLE OF CONTENTS

I dedicate this book to every leader,
past, present, and future,
whose purpose is to make a positive difference,
and whose aim is to contribute to make
our world a better place.

FOREWORD

A re you a small-medium sized company CEO, managing director, shareholder, a private equity executive or a venture capitalist? Do you want to maximise the value of your life-time investment, cash in and enjoy life differently?

Do you believe globalisation benefits everyone except you and your company? Would you like to discover how to ride the wave of globalisation and multiply your company's value?

As an entrepreneur, someone who has grown a business from the ground up, from a micro business into a multinational JV with Molson Coors, one of my priorities is to help and support entrepreneurs and SMEs to thrive. In these uncertain times, you can and must be part of establishing the UK as a trading powerhouse, which is vital for our prosperity. Multiculturalism creates global trade. Diversity drives better decisions. And it is my aim to get better Black, Asian, and Minority Ethnic (BAME) representation in boardrooms across the country.

This is why I am so excited to endorse this book, *SME Globalisation – How to Maximise Your Company Value in a Cost-Efficient Way*. It deals with all those topics, and will help you to find your place on the world stage.

Sandy Damm has been a minority himself for most of his life, living in 6 countries across 3 continents. He is a seasoned hands-on CEO, designing business development strategies around the globe for the last 20 years, holding P&L responsibilities for 12 of those years. He has been involved in turnarounds as well as merger & acquisitions on both the buying side and the selling side. When I met him the first time in 2018, I found his passion for international expansion and global branding to be contagious.

No matter how big or how much your company is worth today, if you intend to multiply your asset value, *SME Globalisation* is for you. In fact, Sandy provides you with bonuses throughout the chapters and guides you step by step how to embrace, ride and thrive the wave of globalisation rather than fearing it.

Lord Karan Bilimoria of Chelsea, CBE, DL
Chairman and Founder of Cobra Beer
President of the CBI – Confederation of British Industry

ACKNOWLEDGMENTS

First of all, I am immensely grateful to **Lord Karan Bilimoria,** entrepreneur, founder, and chairman of Cobra Beer, and president of the CBI, for the honour of this Foreword. His continuous dedication to SMEs, and his consistent promotion of diversity to make organisations stronger, have always been an inspiration to me.

I would like to thank the company owners and top executives for whom I have worked and learned from: **Matthew Carrara, Christian Cuny, Arnaud Houllemare, Mike Kelly, Michael Leipold, Mike Overend, Pascal Paulat, Bernard Schott**, and **John Zarno,** for entrusting me with their businesses and letting me get on with the job. If some have been mentors, all of them have given me the freedom to act with the consequences of failures and successes.

I have a special thought for the late **Larry Klumpp**, whose "More faster" resonates in every boardroom I am involved in, and every shop floor I walk through.

I appreciate everything I have learnt from **Raymond Aaron** and his 10-10-10 Program™, without whom this book would never have been possible. Raymond introduced me to the world of writing and publishing, and gave me the confidence to bring my pen to paper.

I benefited immensely from colleagues, staff, and crews that I had the pleasure to have on board the different ships I captained, and who have all contributed directly or indirectly in making me the person I am today. I do have a special thought for **Stacey Lucas**, **Lorna McCabe**, **Mark Newton,** and **Martin Portwood**, the Sontay Management team I enjoyed building and being part of. I considered them to be the best executive team in the industry.

Thanks to **Andrew Roberts**, former Head of the Executive MBA program at EMLyon, who let me become the youngest executive program participant in history, back in 2003.

I am grateful to **Prof. Stefan Thomke**, Faculty Chair of the General Management Program, and **Ani Kharajian**, Head of Executive Programs at Harvard Business School, for giving me the opportunity to join the GMP to formalise my learning, and prepare myself for my next position to make a difference in the world.

Thank you to my classmates from EMLyon **Executive MBA 2003–2005**, and Harvard Business School **GMP28-29**, from whom I learned as much in class as outside the classroom.

I am extremely grateful to my GMP29 Living Group 16: **Basma Al-Farsi**, **Chivas Alejo**, **Oluyomi Alarape**, **Javid Khan**, and **Martin Krafft**; and our executive coach, **Peter Martel**, for helping me to navigate through a personally and professionally very rough and stormy 2020.

Acknowledgments

As well as my GMP28 Living Group 51: **Paul Granadillo, Feras Houhou, Rahul Kanwal, Dmitry Kostornichenko, Marten Nilsson, Miguel Paredes**, and **Tomo Wanajo**.

I deeply appreciate Harvard Business School's **Prof. Rawi Abdelal's** insights, and his research associate **Sogomon Tarontsi's** authorization to use his figures and charts in Chapter I & II.

I send a warm thank you across the globe to **Monica Kong**, for sharing her experience in managing Chinese teams. (Chapter VII.6)

I appreciate **Jonathan Lord's** sparring partnership, from whom I keep learning the art of strategic recruiting and the value of team building.

Pete Cross, Managing Director of Corintech, for sharing his organisation's Covid experience.

The **DHL Connectedness Annual report** and the **Economist Intelligence Unit teams**, for providing accurate and reliable information weekly, as well as spot-on analysis.

Last but not least, I would like to thank my lifelong friends:

Sir Anthony L. Elliott, a living spirit of Old England, who has honoured me with his friendship for over 20 years, and who still is my number-1 fan.

Teuta Bakalli and **Kam Dehal**, two women who thrive in a man's world, and who are my best albeit most challenging supporters.

Corinna and James Rae, for the warm welcome in their Cotswolds Burleigh Court Manor, where several chapters of this book have been written in an inspiring atmosphere.

And **Michael Swanton**, my brother from another mother, with whom we have done and undone the world in his different backyard sheds, over a few drams (and one or two cigars), for over 15 years.

TESTIMONIALS

As a non-executive director, I have seen Sandy deploying his methodology for driving changes and turning the company into a world player, whilst remaining careful to maintain the sensitive balance between global drives and local requirements.

As an investor, once positioned on the world stage, my investment multiplied far beyond my expectations.

Mike Overend
Non-Executive Director and Venture Capitalist, United Kingdom

In today's challenging economic and political climate, no SME should ignore the opportunities presented by internationally based growth. Sandy has a proven track record of achieving that, using the simple, effective and cost efficient techniques set out in this book.

John Zarno
Chairman of the Sontay Board, United Kingdom

As a board colleague of our industry association, I enjoyed the 3 years working with Sandy, and found the pace and accuracy of his analysis refreshing. His decision making process and drive to make things happen is infectious.

As a customer, I appreciated how effective and sharp his teams were, and how easy it became for my teams to work with them.

Paul Wetherfield
CEO Global Associates, United Kingdom
Highly Commended - IoD London & South East Director of the Year Awards 2017

Sandy is a tremendously competent manager with proven skills in numerous areas needed to grow a business. His transparency and fairness give his shareholders enough confidence to allow him to make significant changes in the business. Sandy laid out a strategy, replaced nearly the entire senior management team, while maintaining profitability and growth. Given his ability to mould the new team, and the fact that he had a strategy which gave the new team a road map, he used these assets to expand and solidify the business. This work was done in a challenging international and multicultural environment, which also tapped into Sandy's strengths. These real results speak directly to his strengths in strategy development, recruiting, team building and leadership. His skills were well applied with perspicacity and humour.

Mike Kelly
President Pion Inc., USA

Testimonials

After a decade of challenging collaboration, Sandy reset the entire relationship. He did what he said, and said what he did. Once terms were agreed upon, he delivered. Over five years both of our organisations benefitted from the strong brand he built, and joint turnover increased by 500%.'

Lee Coffin
COO, UK Electric, United Kingdom

I have known Sandy for almost 20 years, and in whichever organisation he was involved with, he brought direction, clarity and rational decision making, and always increased the generated value.

William Chaux
Serial Entrepreneur, France

Via product enhancement and geographical expansion, Sandy took the company to its next stage whilst maintaining short term profitability by keeping a sensible balance between revolution and evolution. The end result was a delight for the investors.

J. Boyd Murdoch
Venture Capitalist, United Kingdom

Either for large corporations or for SMEs, globalisation has become a fact, shaping the current and future competitive landscape. Globalisation has intensified the competition among companies and industries but also opened opportunities for fast acting organisations. Quick decisions, adopting swiftly to changes, and learning from mistakes and failures have become the keys for success and the pillars for future growth. However, short reaction times are attributed more to smaller companies than large conglomerates, where decision making is often blurred and slowed down by political strife.

Thus, SMEs are in a great position to profit from globalizing markets – Why is it that they do so seldomly? Some of the reasons why SMEs little contribute in globalized markets is based on limited resources and missing knowledge about how to target and tackle overseas markets. This book will support SMEs in overcoming some of these challenges.

David Achermann
CEO, Huba Control, Switzerland

Once Sandy had professionalised his sales organisation in Dubai, his brand became a serious alternative to the big players across the entire Middle East, within just a few years.

Eric Zanolo, Vice President Project Execution Center, Gulf region, United Arabic Emirates

Sandy is an insightful, strategic thinker and an inspiring leader, skilled at assembling high performing teams and delivering ambitious objectives.

Jonathan Lord
CEO & Founder of Lord Search & Selection Ltd, United Kingdom

Sandy's leadership transformed a conventional, UK based company into a global operator. This was especially the case in continental Europe and the Middle East.

His collaborative management style rejuvenated the staff and drove the company to become a customer focused business, which was reflected by dynamic growth in their traditional market and in their becoming an international brand.

The revitalised company he built now has a solid foundation to continue its growth.

Roger Woodward
Industry Strategy Consultant, United Kingdom

During his multiple stays in Asia, Sandy has developed strong relationships with regional business partners across many sectors and industries. In a win-win operating mode, collaborations have benefited all the parties involved throughout the world.

Sebastien Ottaviani
CEO, JEF Industrial Ltd, Hong Kong

Chapter I

What Is a SME?

1. Definitions

Depending on which country you are in, the definition of a small and medium-sized enterprise (SME) varies for either historical or cultural reasons. Some countries offer a different taxation, whether you are a SME or not. The European Union has offered a common definition:

"The category of micro, small, and medium-sized enterprises (SMEs) is made up of enterprises which employ fewer than 250 persons, and which have an annual turnover not exceeding EUR 50 million, and/or an annual balance sheet total not exceeding EUR 43 million."

Source: Extract of Article 2 of the annex to Recommendation 2003/361/EC

Enterprise category	Persons employed	Turnover or	Balance sheet total
Medium	< 250	≤ € 50 m	≤ € 43 m
Small	< 50	≤ € 10 m	≤ € 10 m
Micro	< 10	≤ € 2 m	≤ € 2 m

Source: Eurostat

The UK defines SME as:

"Two out of three characteristics are met: turnover less than £25m, employees less than 250, and gross assets less than £12.5m."
Source: Companies Act SME, UK Department for Business, Innovation and Skills

Whilst the USA defines it as:

"...having gross annual sales below $100 million, fewer than 500 employees, and annual energy bills more than $100,000 but less than $2.5 million. However, in contrast, businesses that mine copper ore and nickel ore can have up to 1,500 employees and still be identified as an SME."
Source: US Small Business Administration agency

This book is written for entrepreneurs, owners, chief executive officers (CEOs), managing directors (MDs), interim managing directors, and presidents (USA), whose focus is on enterprises complying with the €50 million threshold and 250 employees. This also includes divisional CEOs, active in some of the few multinationals organised in conglomerates, who leave a full autonomy to their companies' executive teams, and favour **intrapreneurship**. Another aim of this book would be for demotivated high profiles who are disappointed in their multinational companies (MNC's) jobs, in search of a purpose and incentivise them to jump in the exciting SME world and become richer whilst having control of their own destiny.

2. Where Are They?

Three hundred million SME account for the majority of businesses worldwide, and represent about 90% of businesses, and between 60 to 70% of employment worldwide. They play a major role in most economies, particularly in developing countries. According to the World Bank estimates, 600 million jobs will be needed by 2030 to absorb the growing global needs. This sees many governments around the world making SME development their high priority. In emerging markets, most jobs are generated by SMEs, which create 7 out of 10 jobs.

Europe

The chart on page 6, published by Eurostat, shows a global picture of the European SME landscape, back in 2015:

- Average revenue is €1.16m for an average number of 5.8 employees.
- SME are 99.8% of the companies, generating 55.8% of the revenues, whilst employing 66.3% of the population.
- Germany is by far the most SME dynamic country, generating 22% of the entire EU-28, followed by the UK with 16%, and France with 13%. With little surprise, those 3 countries represent 51% of the EU-28 SME economy.

Number of enterprises, turnover and persons employed and the share of enterprises with fewer
than 250 persons employed, 2015

	Enterprises		Turnover (m €)		Persons employed	
	total	< 250 persons employed %	total	< 250 persons employed %	total	< 250 persons employed %
EU-28	23 500 341	99.8	27 309 775	55.8	137 444 935	66.3
Belgium	602 153	99.9	989 197	65	2 769 085	69.3
Bulgaria	326 219	99.8	121 308	69.9	1 911 916	74.8
Czech Republic	1 001 048	99.8	444 231	56.9	3 591 896	67.6
Denmark	210 726	99.7	479 464	59.3	1 666 048	64.3
Germany	2 408 352	99.5	6 061 400	47.5	28 258 410	62.9
Estonia	68 124	99.7	50 820	77.5	414 763	78.2
Ireland	243 433	:	595 095	:	1 308 019	:
Greece	789 975	:	236 153	:	2 162 572	:
Spain	2 465 540	99.9	1 789 292	62.2	11 109 702	72.8
France	2 908 814	99.9	3 624 869	55.3	14 645 799	61.4
Croatia	146 637	99.7	77 670	60.9	989 598	69.5
Italy	3 683 127	99.9	2 887 615	68.8	14 225 278	78.7
Cyprus	48 329	99.9	25 573	79.9	215 716	83.9
Latvia	109 642	99.8	51 304	77.8	633 450	79.4
Lithuania	186 468	99.8	73 997	68.5	934 440	75.9
Luxembourg	31 926	99.5	151 365	70	255 869	68.3
Hungary	536 610	99.8	277 690	57.1	2 596 236	69.8
Malta	26 059	99.8	18 665	85.1	134 212	79.7
Netherlands	1 092 243	99.9	1 412 433	61.8	5 461 082	65.7
Austria	322 325	99.7	653 111	:	2 742 655	:
Poland	1 606 559	99.8	921 350	56	8 652 063	68.3
Portugal	807 183	99.9	314 227	:	3 007 264	:
Romania	458 122	99.6	263 366	59.1	3 898 199	65.5
Slovenia	134 727	99.8	83 628	68.3	591 340	73.7
Slovakia	429 524	99.9	180 476	56.7	1 502 912	71.8
Finland	229 096	99.7	365 782	56.1	1 454 614	65.6
Sweden	686 433	99.9	811 397	:	3 102 080	:
United Kingdom	1 940 947	99.7	4 348 297	47	19 209 717	53.5
Norway	293 403	99.8	546 504	:	1 610 874	68
Switzerland	142 775	99.2	1 929 684	:	2 737 720	67.1

: not available

Source: Eurostat (online data code: sbs_sc_sca_r2)

eurostat

3. Who Are They?

Let's have a closer look at our two major different or even opposite models, which we could identify under the name of 'Mittelstand' in Germany, and 'Brittelstand' in the UK.

Mittelstand

Concentrated in the south west of Germany—North Rhine West-phalia (Ruhrgebiet), Baden Wurttemberg, and Bavaria—those companies are mostly family owned and transmitted from generations to generations. Their purpose was, post-WWII, to re-build the country and focus on the long term by investing in innovation, machines, land, and people. The main sectors are manufacturing for automotive, electrical equipment, chemicals, and machine tools industries. Over the years, and confirmed by their success, they have reinforced the model and developed it around 5 pillars:

- Strategically, a mittelstand company adopts one niche—one speciality in which it excels—and becomes the undisputable leader. It invests heavily in know-how, technology, high quality machine equipment, and in the qualification of its teams, from top management to shop floor employees.

- After having gained solid market shares in its home market, the company scales up its volumes by expanding internation-ally. Such a scaling up places the company in pole position on the international stage, and whilst being very difficult to catch up with, becomes almost unbeatable.

- A relentless investment in its staff and the apprentice schemes. Whilst other countries decry or mock apprentices for not being smart enough to go to university, Germans learn a job, a craftwork from the age of 15, and keep developing into the company. It is not unusual to see apprentices growing through the ranks and taking control of a factory or a regional sales area.

- An obsession with generational continuity and independence. It is very common that company owners exchange seats at their board, with other family-owned companies, as long as they are not competing with each other. They do exchange good practices and share their network contacts. In a few cases, I have seen a few companies backing each other up financially to pass a rough patch. It is also worth noting that in order to reinforce the cherished independence, buildings and lands are owned either by the company or directly by the family.

- Invested by a social mission: Their success must contribute to the improvement to local social life. Schools, sport clubs, or healthcare are regularly sponsored by companies whose employee's families make use of. This kind of regional eco-system balances the social relation in territories, as well as inside the company. In order to create that precious 'we' feeling, companies have, twice a year, an 'open-day' when employees can bring their families and relatives to visit the facilities and share a beer and a sausage.

There is a proverb about the Mittelstand, saying: The first generation builds it, the second milks it, and the third buries it! Whilst being sarcastic, it does actually describe a genuine situation many Mittelstand companies have to face. The founder is always on a pedestal, and it's rare not to have a chest statue or at least a portrait in the main reception area: He is the person without whom nothing would have happened. Since the company was his baby, he remained involved in everything, and probably died at his desk or in his factory. Picking up from solid foundations, the 2nd generation keeps building up with some long-time servants and experienced team members. Whatever decisions they make, and without really knowing why, they keep sailing in success; a favourable wind blows them up through the 60s to the 80s. When the unprepared 3rd generation arrives in command, the winds aren't as favourable anymore, and the foundations laid by the 1st generation are very far away! I can think of two extremely successful companies where the first concerns, of the two sons of the 3rd generation, are to finance their new Porsches every two years, or in the second case, which paradise will they berth their yacht for the next six months!

More seriously, although unprepared and perhaps with different expectations from life, current 3rd generations are generally smart enough to hire an external CEO, who runs the company for them and looks after the family interests by ensuring the balance between profits, social responsibility, and longevity.

Brittelstand

Like the Mittelstand for Germany, Brittelstand is a massive contributor to the UK economy. However, they operate in a much different mode.

- UK companies operate in a far more short-term orientated strategy. Rather than looking to transmit to the next generation, entrepreneurs would rather exit when deciding to retire, and sell the company to either a larger group, a private equity, or venture capitalists. As an additional example, buildings are leased, and very rarely owned.

- British companies display a much broader diversity of sectors, such as food, retail, or wholesale, whilst their German counterparts are dominated by manufacturing.

- UK companies are not very good at scaling up, and prefer to focus on their home market.

- Surprisingly, coming from a former colonial superpower, the UK is behind on exports outside the EU, with only 17% of their business, whilst their counterparts from Germany, France, and Italy range from 25% to 30%.

Of course, those two models do exist outside the described countries. You will find either profile all over the world. The importance here is not the "where" but the "who," and "how" they are managed. What differentiates them the most is the length of investment (short term vs long term) and underlying strategy (succession vs exit strategy).

4. Limits and Opportunities

Limits

One of the first limits for an SME is its access to finance. Most of the countries have a confederation or trade association, which amongst other services lobbies via politicians, to gain some additional support from banks. The sentence 'cash is king' is certainly true for multinationals in order to seduce shareholders and to keep the stock price up, but it is even more crucial for SMEs to be able to afford further development: innovation or geographic expansion. After the lack of skills, cash is the second most cited obstacle facing SMEs to grow their businesses in emerging markets and developing countries.

Figure 1.3 below demonstrates the importance of the financial institutional architecture of a country in the flourishing of its SME sector. You can see the contrast between European countries, with up to 65% of firms employing below 250; whilst in the USA, it is almost the opposite, with 60% employing over 250 people. I do read this as a direct effect of the source of capital: Venture capital (VC) and private equity (PE) compose 36% of the GDP, and such investors call for aggressive growth. When I talk to PE/VC, the minimum ratio is to multiply an investment by 3 or 4 within 5 years, and so expect rapid growth with heavy returns. If this means changing an entire underperforming executive team after 18 months, so it shall be. The multiplier and return on investment is king, which can leave little space to build for stability across generations.

PE/VC represent only 2 to 4% of source of capital in Germany, Denmark, or in the Netherlands. Those countries' source of capital is bank-based, favouring long-term and stable patterns of ownership and employment, and hence are not pushing to grow and multiply value at any price.

Figure 2. European small firms and US large firms*Note:* Employment by enterprise size. Figures reflect data for 2014 or latest available year.

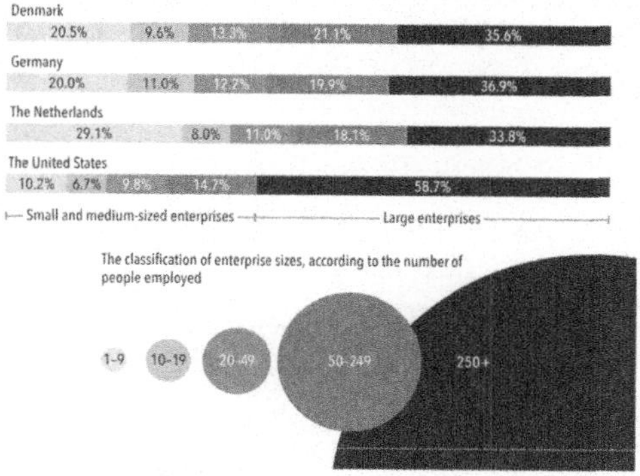

Source: Calculated based on data from OECD, Entrepreneurship at a Glance 2017.

A SME CEO has similar duties to a large company counterpart, whilst having much less resources to carry them out. The more operational he remains, either on the product side or on the sales side, at least he can fulfil his primary duty conducting his company: strategy, HR development, or asset allocation. Typically, the CEO is the strategist, champion, and leader for developing the SME—or, sadly, the prime reason for the business failing. He is also the go-to person for fixing any issue. In many cultures, the CEO is the patriarch who has all the answers, knows everything, and could replace any employee for any work to be done.

The biggest barrier to SME development is the limit of its own CEO's vision and comfort zone. Due to its size, a SME is heavily influenced by him, who often is the founder, owner, and manager of the company. The capacity to expand either technologically or geographically is directly linked to **your** readiness to go out of **your** comfort zone. How able are you to challenge the status quo and to brave the unknown? How many countries don't you export into because it means communicating in a different language, understanding a new culture, or simply dealing with a foreign currency? How often do you see more risks than opportunities in managing foreign teams, shipping issues with customs controls, or simply getting paid?

If you, dear reader, recognise yourself in some of these questions, I sincerely hope this book will help you to push your boundaries. You can then start embracing growth for your company, your teams, and yourself, by becoming a global player.

Opportunities

A SME is the perfect combination of a flexible start-up; you are closer to market reality, customers, and suppliers; and decisions made in the morning can be implemented in the afternoon. Such a setting can attract talents, giving you a higher level of recognition, and a meaningful purpose to share as a team that knows each other more than just as an email address. You will get more exposure to many more areas, and can measure the impact of your contribution. We will review those opportunities in an upcoming chapter.

The latest Covid-19 pandemic has demonstrated how SME can be highly successful by showing agility:

Corintech, an electronics manufacturer, had to cope with an unprecedented increase in demand when the pandemic hit: Medical equipment customers' needs went from 100 units to 110,000 units per month! Managing director, Pete Cross, explains: "We became leaner than ever before, and ran a 30-minute meeting, at 8am every morning, in order to give our teams the rest of the day to focus on actions. We adjusted our level of risk taking, and cut some red tape in order to gain flexibility. In a short discussion, the shareholders and executive team understood which processes could and could not be broken, and implemented immediately."

The sense of emergency and its adrenaline flowed easier through a smaller organisation, and everyone could take ownership and measure its impact to fight the crisis.

How much time would multinational (MNC) teams have spent in meetings, agreeing or not on shortcutting procedures protocols, approving additional suppliers? How much additional exposure could they take without impacting their share price and the quarterly dividends?

5. Differences with Multinational Companies (MNCs)

A key starting point in distinguishing these two business setups is geography. You may operate on a much smaller, local scale, often in a local territory, region in a country, or nationwide. A MNC, by definition, has operations in two or more countries. Its marketplace is broader and more expansive, which presents opportunities for greater customer access, but difficulties in marketing and promotion.

Several areas of business strategy are affected by the scope of your business. SMEs usually emphasise local market strengths and connections with the community. They often use product specialization and personalised approaches to attract target customers. In contrary, MNCs commonly have strengths in distribution, economies of scale, efficiency, and mass marketing. They must decide whether to use a universal business and marketing approach to customise offerings to each country.

Means and available resources are quite different for small companies compared to multinational companies. Small businesses have less money and resources to allocate to certain activities, such as marketing or costly R&D. MNCs need and usually have more money to commit to market expansion, product research, and development and marketing. They do have a wider market to reach with their funds, though.

The system of managing people is more complex in multinational corporations than in small businesses. As a small company, you normally have a smaller employee base. This allows for easier development of a certain work culture and an intimate workplace. Too often, in MNCs, the left hand doesn't know what the right hand does.

Multinational companies have to figure out how to implement HR systems across varying countries and cultures, while maintaining a unified company environment.

In conclusion, I know many SME CEOs and owners who do love to compete against MNCs. You can be faster in product development and launch, and build much closer relationships with all your stakeholders: customers, suppliers and, of course, your own employees. Although your financial power cannot be anywhere near larger corporations, you can be much more cost effective. Flexibility is priceless. In an upcoming chapter, we will see which advantages a SME has, to attract talents in front of an attractive, larger known brand.

Chapter II

What Is Globalisation?

1. A Bit of History

Although commonly believed, globalisation is not a new phenomenon dating from the end of the 20th century. Let's face a few facts:

There is little doubt that the world is in an age of global inter-connectedness, where economic, social, and political events in one part of the world can dramatically impact events in another region. But historians have pointed out the far longer histories of those connections: during the Mongolian Empire, of the 11th to 14th centuries, goods were moved from India to Europe via the first intercontinental overland trade route; and during the era of colonialism, sea trade routes were established by the Dutch and the British East India Companies.

Between 1850 and 1914, the economic integration of the planet continued to accelerate, reaching levels broadly comparable to those of the beginning of the 21st century. The share of international trade between the large industrial countries was about the same in 1890 than in 1990! Towards the end of the 19th century, international openness (trade, capital movements, and immigration) brought about a remarkable convergence of the economies of the Old and New Worlds. Prior to World War I, freedom of capital was largely the rule, linking the financial centres of Europe, the Western Hemisphere, Oceania, Africa, and the Far East. The levels of international financial exchanges were higher, in proportion to the wealth produced, between 1870 and 1914, than between 1970 and 1996. France barely reached the level of the 1930s in 2000. Thus, at the start of the third millennium, we were roughly at the level of the 1914 war.

What has happened since? Between the two wars, barriers to trade, draconian migration controls, prohibitions on the strict surveillance of foreign investments, and fierce currency control flourished. It was not until the 1950s, with the gradual lowering of barriers between countries, that the integration of the economies was able to resume. In 1947, the General Agreement on Tariffs and Trade (GATT) was the first legal agreement between many countries, whose overall purpose was to promote international trade.

So, is globalisation a new fashion? The facts show that it is not; it was kept quiet for decades, that's all. But the perception we have of it today is very different. The rise of the mainstream media, and the spread of mobile networks, internet, and uncontrolled social medias, give the impression of a permanent earthquake.

Looking back to my teenage years, I do identify the key trigger: the fall of the Berlin Wall; later followed by the fall of the Iron Curtain. How could we have built a strong Europe and single market whilst, at its heart, a politically, socially, and economically-divided Germany? The pace at which 12 Central European countries have been integrated, between 2004 and 2007, is largely debatable; nevertheless, Europe now has the biggest single market in the world.

With no surprise, the globalisation seen since the beginning of the 21st century, is stronger, and its consequences on our society are much more widespread and deeper than its previous variations. Chinese and American customers, nowadays, have more means to impose their wishes on a European company seeking to sell its products. Foreign shareholders, via their investments and pension funds on the stock market, control companies and their management whilst being thousands of kilometres away—an unthinkable concept in the years of sailing or steamboats. How does one compare the impact of a single mouse click influencing our way of life and culture, with that of our antique telegraphs; and the current relocations of certain productions, from the countries of the Northern Hemisphere to the Southern Hemisphere, to that of yesteryear? And the attention paid today to the differences in income between countries and social categories, compared to the relative indifference of a century ago?

We have moved from "low frequency globalisation" to "high frequency globalisation." Although we may see a post-Covid-19 slow down, our planet's economic integration is far from over, with its advantages and disadvantages.

2. What is Globalisation?

"Globalisation is the increasing interdependence of world economies as a result of the growing scale of cross-border trade of commodities and services, flow of international capital, and wide and rapid spread of technologies."
Source: Shangqua, 2000

Globalisation as a Paradox

What shall we think about globalisation? What do you, dear reader, think of it? Is it good? Is it bad? Anyone answering these questions is as much right as wrong. We do face a paradoxical situation, and our feelings are split between gender, nationalities, social classes, and religions.

On one hand, globalisation opens the door for global cooperation, trade, and peace, giving the world a platform on which to address, debate, and fix key issues. We feel as being in a virtuous circle: cooperation generates trade, trade generates peace, and peace reinforces cooperation. On average, the global population is safer, better educated, and wealthier and healthier than ever before in history. Some economists even predict that almost 75% of the world shall be at the current UK living standard by 2050. The European continent has been at peace for over 75 years and counting. This has never happened in history.

On the other hand, we do find persistent poverty, increasing economic inequalities, and environmental degradation. Authoritarian regimes take the benefits from economic integration but do not liberalise politics. Extremist groups, such as ISIS or Boko Haram, seek a radical alternative to Western values and democracies, through violence, fear, and death. Even in countries such as the UK or the USA—which are two archetype of globalised economies, and which have benefitted the most from globalisation—we have seen, over the last 5 years, a severe backlash rise, in the form of right-wing populism.

Political Will

Our current level of globalisation would never be where it is now without a shared political will across nations. Globalisation followed the path of history. It took the horror of WWII, and the lessons learned from protectionism programs in the 20s and 30s, for nations to sign, in 1947, the *General Agreement on Tariffs and Trade* (GATT). GATT was an agreement where countries reduced their barriers to trade—tariffs, quotas, embargoes, and other sanctions—and opened up their capital and financial markets. In 1948, the USSR responded to GATT by creating its own *Council for Mutual Economic Assistance* (COMECON). Following the fall of the Berlin Wall, Europeans started to work towards more integration on the founding pillars of free movement of people, goods, services, and money.

In 1995, the World Trade Organisation (WTO) was created. It is the only global international organisation dealing with the rules of trade between nations. At its heart are the WTO agreements, negotiated and signed by the bulk of the world's trading nations, and ratified in their sovereign parliaments. The mission is to ensure that trade flows as smoothly, predictably, and freely as possible. In January 2021, it counted 164 members, representing 98% of the world trade.

The recurrent concept of all these organisations is to provide a table, where nations can sit, exchange, and iron out current and upcoming problems; whilst in the past, they may have invaded or bombed each other. Where there is trade, there is peace. The fewer the trade frictions, the higher the growth.

We shall review other international treaties and single markets in an upcoming chapter.

Economic Integration

The levels of integration are driven by what we call factors of production:

- **Land:** It includes everything involved in the manufacturing of your product, such as natural resources, and the building you rent.

- **Labour:** Human efforts included in your enterprise, directly or indirectly.

- **Capital:** Money and human-made goods used in the production of other goods, such as machines or investments.

The direct reaction of lowering trading barriers is the increase of cross-border exchange levels. Those factors became borderless and are transferable from one nation to another. Each factor of production is a market on his own: Oil, water, industrial property, labour market and, of course, money, are GLOBAL markets nowadays!

Less frictions in trade → economic growth → economic integration → more globalisation

Let's take the example from the automotive industry: Country A and B both manufacture steel and cars, but A can make steel more cheaply, whilst B is more efficient in car manufacturing. Lower tariffs between them gives them the opportunity to concentrate on what they are the best at. Together, they are stronger and more competitive against country C or D. It also leaves consumers better off in either country.

Multinational corporations (MNCs) are the first drivers of economic globalisation. According to the Organisation for Economic Cooperation and Development (OECD), MNCs hold 38% of the global GDP, whilst 30% of the worldwide economy is generated by the top 200 biggest corporations. Over the years, it became more and more apparent how the increasing power and influence of MNCs can influence or shape the economic dynamic of an entire region. This can lead to situations where governments are tempted/incentivised/motivated to lower taxes, wages, and environment controls in order to attract more foreign direct investments (FDI), or simply accommodate MNCs.

Another effect of economic integration is the level of interconnection between economies: Whilst it took months for the 1929 financial crisis to spread across the globe, the 2008 crisis spread almost immediately.

Technological Integration

Technologies have massively contributed to economic growth across nations. Whilst the creation of the internet, in 1991, was the biggest driver, we shall not undervalue the progress made in communication and transportation. According to Shangquan, today's ocean shipping cost is only 50% of what it was in the 30s, the current airfreight 15%, and telecommunication 1%. The older of us may remember the time when, to promote our products, we had to ship catalogues and documents, and it took over a week to go from London to Chicago. I am part of the generation who did send quotes and correspondence via fax, which is better than standard mail, but the response was never as fast as an email. Also, which current sales manager would consider stopping his car close to a telephone box to check in with his office, to ask if there are any messages or phone calls to return, via this same telephone box? Which international businessman needs to be reached via his hotel reception desk, by his family, in order to wish his children good night?

Technologies, for better or worse, have changed and sped up our lives and the globalisation pace. How global would we be without them?

Key Characteristics

In conclusion, we can identify and read globalisation via these 6 different factors:

- Increasing interconnectedness of economic, social, and political affairs across borders
- Increasing dependency of one locality on the events in another
- Compression of time and space through technologies
- Accelerating global interaction through improved transport and communication systems
- Growing collective cognitive shift towards understanding the world as a shared space
- Increasing flow of ideas and goods, with fewer border constraints

Source: Held & McGrew, 2003

But how can we measure it?

3. How Can You Measure Globalisation?

Globalisation can be seen as an amazing opportunity, as well as a massive threat, depending how you look at it. So how can we assess quantitatively and qualitatively its real impact? Since we look at an extremely complex picture, I would recommend the 'PESTE' methodology to easily fact-check measurable economic aggregates.

Political

A country's political engagement into globalisation can be measured by its number of membership to international treaties or organisation, contributions in human resources allocations or funds to humanitarian missions (United Nations Security council), or climate change treaty (2015 Paris agreement), or as basic as the World Trade Organisation (WTO) membership.

The level of existing diplomatic relations is a solid political indicator of how much a country aims to communicate with other states in an equal relation, and play a major role on the international stage.

Economical

The level of economic integration is probably the easiest to identify since it's directly linked to numbers. It measures trade and financial flows between states, with data that are openly published:

Global Trade: The total of imports and exports of goods and services as a percentage of the country's GDP, measure the 'Trade intensity.'

Foreign Direct Investment (FDI): This is simply the amount of investments made by foreign companies or individuals by acquiring assets (companies, real estate) or by establishing businesses (manufacturing, sales organisation, or service provider). The percentage of this amount is the favourite indicator of a country's integration into the global economy.

Restrictions on Trade and Capital Flows: This indicator calculates the percentage of the revenue made on trade tariffs, barriers, and import taxes. This is actually a negative indicator: The higher it is, the less globalised the country is, and the more friction the trade has.

Social

This aggregate measures the level of immigration/emigration, international travel, tourism, cross border information flows, and cultural exchanges.

Immigration stimulates an inflow of new cultures and wealth creation through additional labour into the destination country, whilst feeding back local cultures as well as financial flows to home countries.

The tourism indicators are primarily used as a revenue stream aggregate, and some countries could hardly survive without it: For example, back in 2019, 50% of the Macau's GDP relied on tourists, followed by the Maldives at 33%. Those economical contributions do massively impact the social life, especially in territories where resources other than natural beauty are rare.

We shall not forget that tourism does connect people from different cultures, and a share of it can turn into immigration.

Cross border information flows were easier to measure in the past, with the imports/exports of newspapers, television programs, or international phone calls traffic. In our current internet world, that traffic is quasi invisible to individuals or private organisations.

Technological

Without a shadow of a doubt, internet has been the biggest driver of globalisation: We recorded 4.66 billion users worldwide in October 2020, with 91% accessing it over mobile devices (*Source: Statista*). Surprisingly, this means that less than 60% of the world population have access to it! Countries range from Bahrein (100%), down to Eritrea, at 1%, amongst other African countries in their low 1 digit. This does not include North Korea, where internet is prohibited.

Therefore, the level of technological globalisation of a country can be measured through the share of its population using it. We should not underestimate the traditional phone lines communication, which pre-Covid-19 were still used in more than 35% of international communications!

Technologies also incentivise international cooperation, in sciences and technologies, not to neglect the cultural and political sharing of ideas and movements. Sadly, veracity has been slightly forgotten in that massive, free information sharing.

Environmental

Pushed by younger generations and an increasing international political will, environmental issues have gained traction and relevance over the last decade. Companies recognise more and more the value of ISO 14001 amongst their suppliers, peers, and customers. The real environmental degradation and political response are still difficult to measure. However, some non-governmental organisations (NGOs) such as World Wide Fund for Nature, better known under its WWF acronym, does release its flagship publication, *Living Planet Report*, every two years. It is a comprehensive study of trends in global biodiversity and the health of the planet.

A more direct way to measure environmental impact is to track the economic aggregates of trade of goods that have a significant impact, such as chemical waste, timber, or agricultural products.

4. What Are the Challenges of Globalisation?

We have seen anti-globalisation movements since the end of the last century.

The 2008 crisis has magnified the level of interdependence and vulnerability of the global economy, leading to a proper domino effect.

Fragmentation of Supply Chain

The globalisation of the factors of production: Free flows of capital and labour, added to lower tariffs and falling costs of communication and transport, has led to an unprecedented fragmentation of supply chains across the globe. Global trade between firms and consumers has now been taken over by trade within firms. Let's take the example publicly communicated by Apple, back in 2014, detailing how the iPhone 6 was made. The product is designed in the USA, and contains several hundreds of components produced by 785 different suppliers across 28 countries, before being assembled in China.

This phenomenon is, of course, driven by productivity and cost efficiencies, supporting higher margins and eventually bigger profits. However, such a supply chain is highly exposed to economic, political, or social turmoil. The longer the chain is, the more exposed your organisation is.

You are not Apple, and your supply chain is not as long, but how much exposure to risk do you have? Or are you at the opposite side of the spectrum and are fully integrated, and so lose on cost efficiencies?

Rising Inequality

It is fair to say that globalisation has resulted in uneven developments within and between countries; moreover, it has prompted a steadily increasing anti-globalisation movement. Worryingly, this inequality has kept increasing over the years. For example, in the US, the top 1% earners take home 81x more than the bottom 50%. In the 1980s, this multiplier was around 27!

Business and political leaders (the so-called top 1% or establishment) maintain the core message: 'We ALL have gained, and we ALL will keep benefiting from globalisation.' The distrust keeps rising. Employees' bargaining power, directly and via trade unions, has decreased under the threat of job delocalisation supported by the global labour market.

The establishment failure to reduce inequality has fuelled populism into an anti-globalisation movement in most parts of US and Europe: US election, Brexit referendum, gilets jaunes, etc.

Migration Holding Down Wages

Is it new to see people leaving their home countries to seek new horizons, where their hopes and aspirations can be satisfied? How was America built over the last 500 years? Have we forgotten how the West was won? How was the British Empire conquered? Nowadays, we may not have the same gold diggers aiming for El Dorado, and we don't want to start an opium war anymore, but the aspiration for a new life in a new country remains very human and natural.

Migrant workers contribute to the growth and development of their host country, and often by doing jobs or carrying out duties that local people can't be bothered doing. For example, in April 2020, in the heart of the first wave of Covid19, whilst most of the world was in lockdown, and most of the UK population furloughed, the British government had to charter dozens of flights from Romania into London Stansted to bring in labour to pick fruits in Herefordshire, Essex, and Sussex. I could also talk about the North African immigrants who have spent their (short) life inhaling macadam to build the French highway network in the 60s and 70s.

Migrants, especially unskilled workers, get easily blamed for holding down wages, putting pressure on schools, social services, or housing, whilst sending back a share of their income to their home countries. Migration is a source of tension and is seen as a key element driving inequality.

On a very personal note, I would like to share that since my youngest age, I have been considered a foreigner and a minority in whichever country I was living. In one of my latest assignments, I have also increased the level of foreigners to 25% of our staff, for the greater good of the company. Have I pulled down wages and abused social services, or have we all contributed to the local economy? I humbly believe the latter.

5. 2021 Outlook and Opportunities

As a CEO, you are amongst the people who need to share a vision, a strategy, and a plan based on your environment. I always found the DHL Global Connectedness Index as a rich and useful source of information. Their report is issued annually and is free to download (you can also find it on my website).

10 Keynotes to look for in 2021:

1. After holding steady in 2019, the world's level of global connectedness is set to decline in 2020 due to the Covid-19 pandemic. However, it is unlikely to fall below levels seen during the 2008–2009 global financial crisis.

2. People flows suffered an unprecedented decline in 2020 as nations closed borders to curb the spread of the virus. International travel is on track to fall all the way back to its 1990 level.

3. International trade rebounded strongly after a sharp plunge at the onset of the pandemic. The proportion of global output crossing national borders will decline modestly in 2020.

4. Capital flows were hit harder than trade by the Covid-19 recession, but these flows have also started to recover. Strong policy responses by governments and central banks have helped to stabilise markets.

5. After signs of a slowdown in the globalisation of information flows before the pandemic, international data flows and telephone calls spiked as Covid-19 forced in-person interactions to go digital.

6. Europe claims the top spot as the world's most globalised region, with 8 of the 10 most globally connected countries located there. Europe leads on trade and people flows, while North America is the top region for information and capital flows.

7. The Netherlands is the world's most globally connected country. Singapore ranks second overall, and earned top marks in terms of the size of international flows relative to domestic activity. And no country boasts a more global distribution of flows than the United Kingdom.

8. The list of economies that are seen to punch well above their weight, in terms of international flows, is led by Cambodia, Singapore, Vietnam, Malaysia, and the Netherlands, with regional supply chains a key factor in the performance of Southeast Asian nations.

9. Geopolitical tensions pose a significant threat to globalisation, but for now, there is no strong evidence of the world economy fracturing along regional lines. US-China decoupling, however, has continued to advance.

10. Stronger global connectedness could accelerate the world's recovery from the Covid-19 pandemic, as countries that connect more to international flows tend to enjoy faster economic growth.

BRIC and MINT

Some of you may remember when, in early 2000, some economists predicted that China would take over the US GDP before 2050. The same economists predicted that 4 countries would enter the top 10 powerhouses and disturb the century's long well established order: Brazil, Russia, India, and China (BRIC).

With their 2000 predictions comforted by what are now commonly known facts on BRIC, the same experts strike back and shift their focus on Malaysia, Indonesia, Nigeria, and Turkey (MINT). They predict further that BRIC shall represent 45% of the global economy by 2050, whilst the traditional Western economies from the G7—US, UK, Japan, Germany, France, Canada, and Italy—shall shrink down to 20%.

This would be a major shift where power would be shared by a larger number of actors, a process called 'rebalancing of the world economy.' It implies that countries with lower GDP per capita will experience faster growth, whilst well-established economies shall stagnate. The so-called level of emerging markets shall converge towards developed economies. This is partly linked to the eradication of empires and the failures to build new ones during the 20th century (Germany, USSR, etc.). The flows of trade, capital, and people are currently much more diversified than when they were concentrated through empires.

Aren't we living in interesting times?

The below chart illustrates the evolution of the balance of powers over the last 150 years:

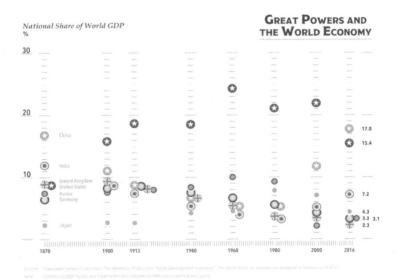

Source: R Abdelal / S.Tarontsi (Harvard Business School)

- 1870 is dominated by China and India, closely followed by the UK.
- The 2 World Wars have built up the US hegemony until very lately.
- Independently from growth or recession, European countries share have declined over the period.
- When political leaders from either side of the Atlantic say they want to make their 'country great again,' it probably means to bring us back into 1870 or 1960 configuration.
- 2016 shows a clear trend of the BRIC, led by China, with the US passing 2nd for the first time in 120 years.
- Where may MINT be in 10 and 20 years' time?

Chapter III

Design a Global Strategy

1. The Strategy Review Process™

By definition, *strategy* is a plan of action designed to achieve a long-term or overall aim. Depending on the organisations, strategies can be conceived in massive ivory towers over months, or just in the pub in an after-hours session. Some family-owned companies can even be found elaborating strategies over the weekend barbecue. Too many SMEs that I have been talking to over the years, believe strategies are something for multinationals, and don't have much use in their world. Strategy is like an objective: Not having one is the safest way to miss where you want to be in the long term.

First of all, you and your board must decide where you want to be in 5 years' time: Nowadays, 5 years is commonly accepted as long term. The strategy will be built towards this long-term goal, overall aim, and vision. Recently, I spoke to a low FTSE250 listed company, and after 20 years of stagnating share price, the board grew ambitions and decided to double/triple in size by going 'global.' Seven out of nine members of this board are non-executive, British, white, male, and 65+, for whom the first priority is to preserve the status quo and keep doing things the way 'we have always done them.' How much chance does this company have to drastically change its course, whilst keeping repeating the same things and doing them the same way? How much time and energy would the executive team burn, debating the need for changes? How much time would it take for the executive team to feel a total demotivation? This real life example demonstrates how important it is to have a common and shared vision. There is no good or bad project here, and there isn't anything wrong with running a lifestyle business with a family-owned mentality: paying your mortgage, children's universities, and the sailing boat. To succeed, it is absolutely crucial that this vision is shared and accepted by everyone, so the entire organisation can align behind it and row in the same direction. This starts in the boardroom and, as a CEO and/or owner, this is your primary responsibility.

Once the vision is set, shared, and accepted, you and your board are ready to enter *The Strategy Review Process™*. As a team, you will decide how to deliver by:

- Determining an accurate and structured strategy.
- Identifying, developing, and strengthening your key success factors (KSF).
- Investing in new products, machines, or services if necessary.
- Organising your entire supply chain accordingly.
- Building the necessary teams, competences, and keys to motivation.
- Allocating the necessary resources, and adapting your financial structure.

The end product of this process is your *Strategy Document™*, which basically becomes your bible for the reach of your long-term vision, with a detailed plan for the upcoming year. Each executive team member can then make his decisions in accordance with the agreed plan. Should questions or arguments arise during the year, decisions can rationally be made by referring to this document, either between executive members or between the CEO and his shareholders.

As a format, I would recommend you sit your entire executive and non-executive team for 1 to 2 days, full time, in an isolated environment, away from the everyday operative life. It not only gives you the required insights for strategic reflexion, but also contributes to build bounds within the team on a more social side.

The quality of this Strategy Review Process™ will depend on the level of preparation and effort you and your team have put in. By experience, it takes 3 weeks of preparation (on and off) in order to gather, analyse, and create a meaningful diagnostic. This work is a prerequisite and should be shared between members.

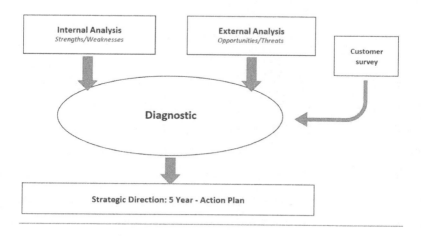

2. SWOT: Internal Analysis

The SWOT analysis (Strengths – Weaknesses – Opportunities – Treats) is your first step into your strategy design. You and your team will conduct a review of your core and non-core competences, as well as the assessment of how you allocate your resources. In order to keep it as accurate as possible, it must be realistic, fact-based, and using all the existing available data. You must avoid pre-conceived belief and self-praise between your members. You will find a SWOT template downloadable on this book's website.

Strengths

You analyse what your organisation is good at and what differentiates you from your competition: It can be anything from a loyal customer base, high level of cash, unique know-how or technology, or simply a strong brand.

Weaknesses

This is basically what you are not so good at. What prevents you from performing at a higher level? What are your sales prevention departments? This should enlighten the areas in need of improvement and what to do to increase your competitiveness: no recurring business, lack of capital or debt, easy to copy know-how, or weak brand.

The basic question to ask yourself: What are we good at, and what are we not so good at? To ensure you cover all the aspects of your company, I do recommend to follow the 5Ms technique.

- **Market**

  Customer split? Too large? Which market sector do we cover? Geographical market?
  Product portfolio? Product balance? Price levels?

- **Men**

  Teams' workload? Level of qualifications? Need for training, mentoring?
  Do we have high flyers? How do we retain them?
  Succession plan for key people?

- **Means**

  How efficient and updated is our IT architecture? ERP? MRP? CRM?
  How much effort do we invest in R&D? International sales field presence?

- **Money**

  How are we optimizing our cash? How are we using it?
  Conduct a complete review of all your ratios, and benchmark them towards your competitors.

- **Machines**

  Age of equipment? Have we under/over invested in manufacturing machines? IT equipment?

3. SWOT: External Analysis

The external analysis is the screening of your environment, over which you have little control. However, even with no control at all, it can give you indications of how you can shape your organisation in order to surf the wave and make the best of it.

Opportunities

This refers to favourable external factors that could give an organisation a competitive advantage: a wave to ride. For example, one of your competitors goes bankrupt; your country enters into a trade agreement, opening doors to a new market; or there are new regulations, creating new markets.

Threats

This refer to factors that have the potential to harm you and your organisation. Identifying them through this analysis will help you first to be aware of them and, more importantly, to build defences. You may even be able to turn some of them into an advantage. Common threats include things like rising costs of materials, new competitors entering your market, or rising trade tariffs, making you less competitive on the international stage.

You may want to use the PESTE screening methodology:

- **Political**

    Membership in free trade agreements
    Tax laws

- **Economical**

  Market size
  Existing market/accessible market
  Currency exchange rates
  GDP ratios in your target countries

- **Social**

  Cost of labour
  Demographics (age distribution)
  Employment laws
  Cultural attitudes/lifestyle trends and how they can affect your customers

- **Technological**

  How much could new technology affect our business?

- **Environmental**

To have the analysis as comprehensive as possible, I would recommend that every team member does this exercise on his own, and one person (you) compiles all the inputs into the chart. Once you have reviewed your organisation and your environment, you will be in a position to combine your:

- Strengths and your opportunities, and to reinforce them in order to gain a higher level of competitiveness.
- Weaknesses and threats, which will make it apparent where you are the most vulnerable and most likely to get hit first.

4. The Strategy Document™

In parallel of your team working on the SWOT exercise, you should conduct the global data review of your organisation. Like a car, you dismantle every year to the last bolt and nut; you go deep inside your organisation to complete the first section of your strategy document. These homeworks are like a data room, where auditors come once a year, or when an acquisition due diligence process is conducted: long, meticulous, very detail orientated, and necessary for a successful process. The better the data, the better the output and the result of this entire exercise.

Once the first part of your Strategy Document™ is set, you and your team are ready to shape the future of the company.

5. Diagnostic

Once you have analysed every possible element of your organisation and environment, you will have made apparent your key success factors (KSFs) and understand why you are successful. The results of your external customer survey will confirm or correct your conclusions.

A few years ago, I was involved in such a strategy exercise with a British manufacturer. Their market position in their home market was solid, but they struggled to be successful outside the UK and Ireland; the combination of both countries weighted 80% of their total revenue. Indeed, several years of commercial investments in North America, India, and Australia generated only around 2.5% of their total revenue, which was disappointing. When we explored their KSFs and why the company was so suc-

1. Key target of the current year review
      1.1 Key Target 1
      1.2 Key Target 2
      1.3 Key Target 3
      1.4 Key Target 4
2. Financial review
  2.1 Sales
  2.2 Gross Margin%
  2.3 Overheads
  2.4 Profit impact of changes
  2.5 Financing costs
  2.6 EBIT
  2.7 Breakeven sales level
  2.8 Forex Impact
  2.9 Balance sheet

3. Sales review
  3.1 Review by geographical pole
    3.1.1 Area 1
    3.2.2 Area 2
    ....
  3.2 Market and Competitor Analysis
    3.2.1 Market sizes and market shares
    3.2.2 Competitors financial assessment
    3.2.3 Home country competitive analysis
    3.2.4 Europe competitive analysis
    3.2.5 Middle East competitive analysis
    ... (other regions if applicable)
    3.2.6 Competitor 1
    3.2.7 Competitor 2
    ... (full list)
4. Product review
  4.1 Product segmenting
    4.1.1 Segment 1
    4.1.2 Segment 2
    4.1.3 Segment 3
  4.2 Product positioning and pricing
  4.3 Pareto analysis by product lines
    4.3.1 Product line 1
    4.3.2 Product line 2
    ...
  4.4 Product development
    4.4.1 New products
    4.4.2 Product discontinuations
    4.4.3 Product cost saving plan

cessful in UK and Ireland, everyone internally and externally was unanimous about the quality of the products, and moreover about the first class service:

- For any order received before 3pm, the customer receives his goods before noon the next day.
- A great commercial relationship with the internal sales team, able to give product recommendations and instant availability information.
- A best-of-industry technical support, where customers called from site to get live guidance for commissioning products.
- The customer survey confirmed how much people appreciated to have direct access to their contact persons through direct phone lines rather than using e-mails or switchboards.

Now, how much of these KSFs can be duplicated to North America, India, or Australia? None! The company was obviously comfortable addressing former commonwealth countries; whilst there is nothing wrong with following cultures, you cannot ignore geography and time zones. At that time, the company was part of the biggest single market in the world, where all of the mentioned KSFs, after a few adjustments, could be easily duplicated!

The executive team was composed of very successful, experienced, and smart business people; the everyday life just made them lose sight of the obvious. The purpose of the Strategic Review Process™ is to force people to step back from their everyday busy life, and incentivise them to reflect more than usual on how things operate.

Once your diagnostic is laid down and confirmed by the external survey, you are ready to build your 5-year plan to deliver your vision.

6. Build Your 5-Year Plan

When I build a 5-year plan, I like to set it on the magic number 4: 4 key targets—4 pillars on which the entire company strategy will be built, to deliver the 5-year vision, supported by a solid action plan.

You MUST set easy key performance indicators (KPIs), which will be the measure of your progression towards your vision and targets. Typical KPIs for profit and value drivers can be found in Chapter X.

As stated earlier, this Strategy Document™ is now your bible, and every team member can act, behave, and make his own decision in accordance with the agreed plan. When, during the year, an unusual question comes up or a tough decision has to be made, the simple referral to this document shall enlighten and guide everyone. Although confidential, this document can also be produced to your auditors or your bank. Should you request an influx of cash, your banker will feel more comfortable to lend you money, for several reasons. First, he will understand what and why you need it for; second, he will have a full understanding of your financial situation and projection; and third, he will rarely have seen such a comprehensive analysis at a SME level, and will trust you to know what you are doing and where you are going.

```
5.    Operations
      5.1 Factory Change and Investment
              5.1.1 Factory improvements
              5.1.2 ...
              5.1.3 Planned Capital Expenditure
      5.2 Business systems
      5.3 Organisational changes
              5.3.1 Factory
              5.3.2 Purchasing
              5.3.3 Sales
6.    Strategic Direction
      6.1 Vision
      6.2 Sales
              6.2.1 Area 1
              6.2.2 Area 2
              ... (full list)
      6.3 Marketing
      6.4  Product sales activities
              6.4.1      Product line 1
              6.4.2      Product line 2
                         ...
      6.5  People Development

7   Key Targets
      7.4  Key Target 1 – Pillar 1
      7.5  Key Target 2 – Pillar 2
      7.6  Key Target 3 – Pillar 3
      7.7  Key Target 4 – Pillar 4
```

In a later stage, this document can of course also be produced to potential buyers. A potential investor or new owner will have the exact same comfortable feeling as a banker.

Chapter IV

Develop a Global Brand

IV

1. Your Brand, This Hidden Gem

Adored or criticised, your brand is, above all, a business development tool. It does not replace marketing, but once built, it constitutes a strategic competitive advantage. It is a source of profit and enhancement of your business. This is why all economic players today develop brands, from manufacturers to distributors, from generic drugs to low cost airlines. Brands stand for much more than products or services: They attract interest of countries, cities, sports teams, or television programs.

This chapter invites you to understand the logic of branding, with its constraints, costs, and associated risks. You will learn how to play its rules to your advantage.

Although I was fortunate enough to attend the best executive programs, in the best universities in the world, my best ever "branding masterclass" was revealed to me during a visit of the World of Coca-Cola museum, in Atlanta, Georgia (USA). During the entire tour, you come closer and closer to the brand via your five human senses. First of all, you are greeted with a drink (*taste*), and then as you walk through, you learn that the bottle had been designed in a way that it could be recognised by the *touch*; then it is explained that the sound, when you open a can, is fully part of the customer experience too (*hearing*). The visual of the brand doesn't need to be introduced (*view*): From Piccadilly Circus in London, to the biggest sport events in the world, everyone has seen the white curve and writing on the red background. On the last stage of your visit, you can enjoy a scent discovery experience of all the different variants existing, or which have existed, under the banner. This fulfils your last sense: your *smell*.

Your SME is obviously not Coca-Cola, and does not have such finance or marketing firepower. Multinationals spend millions on advertising, marketing, and public relations (PR) to build brand recognition of their company or their products/services. They throw money at their target customers, using television, radio, magazines, and the internet. The strategies for branding are the same in SMEs, but the scale, costs, and a few of the tactics change.

Strangely enough, very few SMEs capitalise on their brand. Once, I have even come across one who did not dare to put their own brand on their own products, fearing it would cost them all their business! If this is your case too, and you are ashamed of putting your name on your products, perhaps you shouldn't sell them— or better yet, don't even produce them.

A strong brand makes you better than your competition. Even if your product is absolutely the same as every other product, branding makes it special. Your product becomes the first product a customer thinks about when thinking about making a purchase. So, how can you build your brand and make it an experience that will keep your customers faithful and gaining more than from your competitors?

2. Anatomy of a Brand

Your *brand identity* can be identified, built, and strengthened on the following pillars:

Security

Buyers hate insecurity. This is why the first level of the brand is the reduction of perceived risks. It increases with the price, the technicality of the product, or the importance of the problem to be solved. This is why patients are attached to their brand of paracetamol: They go for the one that usually relieves their headaches immediately. In the medical or food sectors, there will always be a greater source of concern. Big, well-known brands **never** compromise on quality.

Promise

Your customers expect you to deliver what you promise. If your brand is associated with high quality, high price, and 1st class service, you have to deliver. When you don't, you disappoint your customer and devaluate your brand. This brand promise can be different through your product portfolio: You can have a range of premium, mid-range, and low-cost items. Each of them will have a different performance, can have a lower service rate and, obviously, a different pricing. Your brand has to deliver the promise, even scaled accordingly.

A strong brand always stays faithful to its promise. It is your contract, binding you to your customers. Your customers do live in a real world, and mistakes do happen, even for big brands. Just keep in mind: It is not the mistakes that make or break your brand; it is the way you react to it and how you deal with it. If you have identified a serial fault in production batches, be brave enough to organise a recall campaign. It will be costly, but your brand will become stronger.

Never forget that you are the number 1 ambassador and ultimate guardian of this promise.

Experience

Your brand must be associated with an easy-to-use feature for the end user, as well as for all the intermediary who come in touch with it. Do your products have a differentiator factor that you can deploy across your ranges? A technical feature that becomes your brand signature is a powerful way to retain your customers and build up your brand. There is no coincidence that larger organisations create Director of Customer Experience positions. The purpose is to strengthen the entire experience of the product, as well as around the product: order processing, lead times, technical support, warranty, etc.

Self-Image

This is also called your 'badge.' Tell me which brand you use, and I will tell you who you are. Let's consider some examples of mega brands. Are you Coca-Cola or Pepsi? McDonald's or Burger King? Adidas or Nike? Android or iOS? Rolex or Omega? Mercedes or BMW? Whatever your choice is, you do feel like you are in a club, or part of a band, and it does fill your need of belongingness. In my experience, once you are on one side, you rarely switch over. Your SME is obviously not Coca-Cola or Nike; however, this pillar should not be neglected, and you becoming the Coca-Cola of your industry will give you an advantage and value over all your other competitors.

Should you have an aging customer base, you must consider refreshing your brand: Reinvent and target towards the next generation. As your younger customers adopt your brand and join your club, the stronger your brand will shine, and the stronger and longer lasting your customer base will be.

Ethical

The ethical dimension to branding is a relative new dimension, enforced by the rise of the Environmental, Social, and Governance movement (ESG). You can't ignore it any longer, and your brand must be associated with it. I meet more and more SMEs whose multinational clients ask for their ISO14001 certificate. You can switch towards recyclable packaging, have solar panels on your facility's roof, or switch your company car fleet to electric vehicles. If your brand contributes to make the planet a better place, the younger generation will adopt you...for life.

3. The Art of Thinking Global and Acting Local

"Think global, act local" is a well-known and definitely overused expression. Everyone believes they are good at it, but very few actually are. One of the key challenges of building your global brand is to balance global standardisation with local customisation. This balance is very different from company to company, industry to industry, and country to country. The magic formula is to keep a consistency in your global positioning, whilst leaving your local teams to adapt in pricing, distribution, and marketing to address the local needs.

The global level is also where you define the essence of the brand and its positioning. Ideally, your brand creates an emotional connection to customers that is borderless. If you are consistent with your brand essence, you can make minor adjustments to your positioning in a targeted market, without starting to dilute it.

The local level is where you must accept regional rules, sales channels, and pricing. When penetrating a new market, having your pricing strategies right is the most important decision you can make locally. You will be influenced by very diverse factors, such as local competitors that you may not have in other countries, or simply a different potential customer base.

When It Goes Wrong

Fifteen years ago, Barclays Bank adopted a highly selective positioning in France: Clients needed a minimum of €100,000 deposit or €75,000 annual income to be accepted. Whilst in the UK, Barclays maintained its 'bank for everyone' position. This positioning gap was not sustainable, and led to the sale of this highly selective business to another private banking group.

When It Works

Let's consider two of the most powerful brands in the world: Coca-Cola and McDonald's.

When you find yourself abroad, in a foreign country, where even the words are written in a different alphabet, what are you most naturally looking for? You are naturally attracted to what you know the most in an unknown world. So, you go for McDonald's or for a Coca-Cola. Why? Because you know what their promise is, what you will get, and how they will deliver. It may even make you feel 'at home,' because this is where you went for a meal as a child, and where you take your children when you actually are 'at home.'

This is the power of globalisation: one brand, one promise, wherever you experience the product.

Now, if we look at the local level, even those two superstar brands have to adapt locally. For example, McDonald's had to invent a hamburger with no burger, in countries where beef is not eaten. Coca-Cola, facing too high transportation costs, is forced to bottle or can their drinks locally, using local water. The local water, mixed with the Coca-Cola magic powder, is the only difference from country to country.

If those two superstars cannot afford to impose their brand, and must still respect and play by local rules, do you believe your SME can?

4. Make Your Brand Shine High

Create Your Identity

Make sure your brand or company name says what you do. For example, *Brown Ltd.* doesn't say much; the trick is to call your company *Brown Fencing,* to describe what your business is. You can still decide to add either *Brown* or *Brown Fencing* as a logo on your product. It is also important that your name can be read and pronounced in as many countries and languages as possible.

When it comes to your corporate design, mind your visual identity. Be mindful with the colours and how people can make associations. For example: Orange is the colour of a famous low-cost airline company. Do you want to be identified as a low-cost provider? If yes, adopt orange; if not, don't!

Corporate design is a long-term investment, and I invite you to hire an external professional to deliver the concepts and its implementation.

Deploy

Your website is your first shop window, and its main purpose is to attract more customers. Once you have finalised your visual identity and corporate design, a web designer can develop your website with all the best features: search engine optimisation (SEO), to make sure your name makes it up the list for any search in your activity and sectors. The more visitors you have, the more you go up the list. So if you start having your website in more languages, you will attract more visitors. In how many languages is your website today? How many visitors per month do you have?

Upgrade by Association

An easy way to grow your brand is to associate it with stronger brands. Next to which higher authority can you display your brand?

The most straight forward way to expose your brand is to be present with the biggest distributor of your target market. It will not only associate you with a market authority who resells your products, but it will also give you free exposure to all of its customers. Another option is a key account customer who agrees to be used as a reference. For example, if you are a mechanical parts manufacturer, how much would your brand be upgraded by if you mention Airbus or Jaguar Land Rover as your customers? If you are a supplier to the retail sector, how much does it up-brand you to be present in Harrods?

Become an Authority

How can you become a market authority in your sector? Do you have a specific technical savoir-faire? Does your industry have a lack of know-how and training programs?

You may consider to start your own training sessions: first, for your own employees; then for your customers, and eventually for all the industry actors. This is a longer process and can require heavy investments. However, here again, you can decide to keep it lean: rent a room and its video equipment; hire a professional trainer; invite your customers. You are left with producing the contents, which is a one-off cost for material that you can update regularly. Further down the road, you could seek professional or official certification for your programs. Once you ramp up your volumes, you could even have your own P&L— your academy is born!

What better way do you know to make your brand a market authority?

Become Local

Acting local means being on the ground. Visit, analyse, understand, and embrace local culture. Your customer base must feel how much you and your entire organisation genuinely want to be part of it. Only then can you start building long-term success, and become a challenger or a local market leader.

What does a customer expect from a local supplier? A local address, local phone numbers, local language speaking contact persons, website and catalogue in his language, and a price list in his currency. Customers also expect a frictionless order process: no paperwork or import duties.

With technology nowadays, you can fulfil and deliver all those expectations! It is very easy for you to be seen as a local provider, especially in countries that are part of the same free trade area as you. (See Chapter V). You can rent an address, have a local phone number, and subcontract a local payroll for your local teams, for less than £300/month. The translation of your website, catalogues, and price lists are a large but one-off cost. To make a success out of it, you will need multicultural teams, to whom you can give freedom and ownership of this implementation. They can be based wherever you like (time zone permitting), and can still look local to your customers.

5. Social Media

Having a social media identity is no longer optional for your SME in today's world. Too many CEOs or SME executives still believe this typology of marketing is only for multinationals! How often do I hear: *"Our customers know who we are, and they know where to find us,"* or *"Our customers don't use social media, so why should we?"*

If you don't have the know-how in-house, you can either hire a part-time resource as a freelancer, appoint an agency that does it for you under the form of a retainer, or build up your own capacity and train your existing teams. Depending on how active you want to become, and on the nature of your business, you can scale your resource allocation from 5 to 15 hours per week. In my experience, this is the average for SMEs.

Where?

Which platform to use and be active on, depends on your target audience and your business model. If you are in a B-to-B sector, you must be active on LinkedIn, since it draws 80% of the leads. If you are in B-to-C, prioritise Facebook! If your target is the younger generation, focus on Instagram and Snapchat! The unavoidable social media remains Facebook, with its 1.85 billion daily active users.

Why?

As in any traditional marketing or advertisement campaign, you do need to define what your goals are. Do you want to generate more sales? Build up your brand awareness and recognition? Build up a community? Give customers support and enhance their experience with you? The means and action will differ depending on your expectations, and you will end up with a combination of different platforms.

What?

A natural way to generate contents is to make short videos about how to use your products. Depending on their level of technicality, some installers or users may just need some help when onsite. YouTube is the best place to create your own company channel and to publish a database of your 'How to Use' videos. Share success stories, publish pictures of referenced projects your company has won, and make yourself an authority by beating your competitors on the social media battlefield.

How?

A value driver of social media is the number of followers directly linked to your number of posts. Here too, your intent has to be meaningful in order to be taken seriously by your target audience. The minimum is to post ONCE per day. A recent study has demonstrated that only half of SMEs publish daily. Twenty-five per cent post once per week, whilst the last 25% post once per month or even less. The key to generate traffic is to link all your profiles with each other, and generate more visits, more followers, and build up your community. Your number of followers are directly linked to the power and the value of your brand. Not all your followers must be customers; however, you may win them over through those channels!

The more languages and countries your followers are based in, the more global your brand becomes, and the more your brand value increases. Ultimately, this is the most cost efficient way to increase your company value.

Chapter V

Position Yourself as a Global Player

1. Level of Internationalisation

efore addressing the different regions, we should shortly review the options you have to position your company on the international stage. You have to decide to which extent and to which exposure you want to do it. You only need to keep in mind that the more exposition you want to gain, the costlier it becomes.

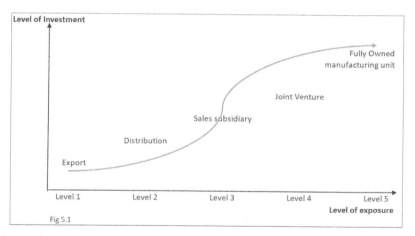

Fig 5.1

Level 1 – Export

You sell to international customers who found you either via direct contact or via social media. You may have a part-time or full-time, internal or even external, sales force that does dynamic prospection. This stage also includes exhibiting on foreign trade shows, and attending international conferences. There is a direct relation between you and the customer. From a transaction perspective, there is a direct flow of goods and capital between both of you: He orders, you deliver, he pays you. Should there be a border between you and him, administrative and financial import burden must be taken care of by one of the parties.

Level 2 – Distribution

You have a local distributor in your customer market. All the import duties are taken care of, between your partner and you, taking away the burden from the customer. Although the customer may know you directly, from a transaction perspective, he buys from your distributor and has all the benefit from buying locally (currency, payment terms, local law, etc.). The distributor takes the payment risk, but you pay him a margin for doing the intermediary.

In some countries, you could have a sales representative paid on commission, leaving you taking care of the flow of goods and capital. This is an extremely popular model in the USA.

Level 3 – Sales Subsidiary

A sales entity in a foreign country, with a local sales force, is a clear statement of your intent to be taken seriously in the market. The core message perceived by customers is reassurance of you being close and providing a first class service, starting with a high delivery performance. This may mean having local inventory to absorb the import burden. However, if based in a common market, you could potentially deliver from your factory into the country of your customer, without having him noticing any additional delay or burden. The market sees you as a local player and cares little where you manufacture.

Level 4 – Joint Venture (JV)

In some situations, providing local support from your head office is too much of a stretch, especially for target markets who are several hours outside your time zone. In order to show local responsiveness, which could be anything from technical support to local product adaptation, you may come to a stage where you will need to make a direct investment. The financial risk and the thin spreading of your management might be a step too far, and so you may consider the option of a local partner with whom you co-invest in a local operation. This operation could serve only the target country, or an entire region. Lately, I was talking to a UK based manufacturer of ventilation equipment, and in order to respond to local market specifics, they established a JV with a South Korean manufacturer. The JV is also the sales subsidiary for the entire Asia-Pacific region.

Joint ventures are like a marriage: They are always very tempting; each party has its rosy glasses on, and everything runs smoothly...until it doesn't anymore. And this is when a painful divorce starts burning the precious commercial and industrial efforts made over the years. The very few JVs that I have actually seen working and ending well, were the ones who had a clear exit strategy: The collaboration was limited in time, and either party knew under which conditions the split could happen. I remember a French manufacturer who entered a JV with a UK distributor. After 3 years, once the business level permitted, the manufacturer took the business in a newly created, 100% owned sales subsidiary. Was the distributor happy about it? Probably not. But the exit conditions (human, financial, and material) were agreed on day 1, and so was the valuation method of the exit fees (actually the buyout clause). A JV can be the last step to the ultimate level of global exposure.

Level 5 – Fully Owned Manufacturing Entity

Investing in 100% manufacturing is indeed the highest level of global exposure. It could either serve only the local market or become a unit specialised in a certain product range, which you would then sell globally, including back into your home market.

Whatever level of internationalisation you intend to achieve, you will reduce the risk by investing in a common market area, to have all the benefits of free trade, and serve the largest base of customer possible. Don't forget: By being present in one member state, you will have free access to all the other member state markets. We will now explore the largest single markets in the world, with their benefits and indication of how to approach them.

2. Europe

The European Union (EU) has the biggest single market in the world, with the highest level of integration.

Foundation: 1993 **Population:** 450 mio **Area:** 5 mio km²	**Members:** 27 EU Member states + 4 non EU Member states **GDP:** $20 trillion **GDP/capita:** $40,000

Source: The Economist – 2020 World in figures

Economic

The European Single Market allows free trade between the 27 member states of the European Union and 4 non-member states: Norway, Iceland, Lichtenstein, and Switzerland. The core foundations of the single market are based on its 4 freedoms: the free movement of capital, goods, services, and labour. As of 2020, 19 member states have adopted the € euro, the single currency that remains optional to any member. One could argue that some of the members have been granted membership (far) too early, or that it was simply a bad idea.

The EU also has 44 preferential trade agreements with individual states or regional trading blocs, covering a total of 77 countries, from Asia to South America via Africa. By the time I write this chapter, an 'oven-ready' agreement with Mercosur will still have to be ratified in Brussels. You can download the full trade agreement listing on my website.

By establishing a company in any of those 31 EU countries, you will not only gain free access to all the 31 markets, but also the 46 other non-EU countries covered by the preferential trade agreements.

Culture

Although trading is frictionless, you will face language and culture barriers. Indeed, Europe is called the 'Old Continent' for a reason: The European single market hosts the most diverse cultures and languages in the world—24 different languages binding Latin, Anglo-Saxon, Slavic, and Nordic cultures.

Where to Go?

Notwithstanding being a member, each state still has its sovereignty to attract foreign direct investment (FDI), either from inside or from outside the single market. Depending on the nature of your investment, and number of jobs you plan to create, some countries may offer you fiscal stimulus on employment taxes, or reduced corporate tax for the first few years, whilst some others may allocate you subventions to implement production or logistic operations.

For a logistic platform on the continent, the Netherlands seem to have the biggest assets, due to their geographic position with road networks to easily access Belgium, Germany, and France, as well as the Nordics via sea. Rotterdam is the biggest and busiest port in Europe, and an ideal gateway for imports from Asia. It runs 16% of the entire EU traffic. A close backup to Rotterdam is Antwerp, 100km (62 miles) south, and although in Belgium, the transfer between ports is frictionless. The combination of both ports gives you access to 28% of the entire European maritime traffic. As we have seen in Chapter II, the Netherlands are the most globally connected territories, and English is widely spoken, and not only in the business world.

For a sales entity, you may decide to pick a country that has your biggest market potential and the lowest competition barriers to enter. Once you have gained solid market shares, it gives you a base to develop neighbour markets. France could be one, thanks to its impressive rail network and high-speed trains (TGV). From Paris, you are less than 2 hours from Strasbourg in the east and Germany, less than 2 hours from Brussels (Belgium), 2.5 hours from Bordeaux on the South West coast, 3 hours from Geneva

(Switzerland), and 3.5 hours from Marseille on the South East coast. Amsterdam (Netherlands) remains 3 hours, and with the Eurostar, you can be in London within 2.5 hours.

For many of you, Germany might be the biggest market on the continent, which most likely means you have local manufacturers to compete with. If this is the case, you will struggle to get a solid market share. Germans like to buy locally manufactured products, and a regional sales office with a local sales team won't be enough to penetrate the market. Having myself been in this situation in several different industries, I had discussions with potential customers and, when asking what needs to be done in order to do business together, the answer was: *'Deutsch werden,'* which means 'Become German.' In other words, if you are really serious about Germany, I strongly advise you to set up a factory or possibly buy a local operation. An intermediary solution could be a JV, as seen in the previous section. The 'Made in Germany' stamp will reinforce your hand in the entire single market, especially in the Eastern European region.

3. Middle East

Saudi Arabia, United Arabic Emirates, Oman, Kuwait, Qatar, and Bahrain form the Gulf Cooperation Council (GCC). This union aims for closer economic and political coordination to counterbalance a too big and sometimes annoying neighbour: Iran.

Foundation: 1981 **Population:** 65 mio **Area:** 2.6 mio km²	**Members:** 6 **GDP:** $1.7 trillion **GDP/capita:** $35,000

Source: The Economist – 2020 World in figures

Economic

Highly dependent on oil and gas, the entire region has seen an incredible economic boom over the last 15 years whilst investing in tourism, building and construction, manufacturing, retail, and more importantly, financial services. Although established in 1981, the GCC only properly launched their common market in 2015, with the free movement of any GCC citizen, and an almost free movement of goods and services. The council has a project of single currency, but it has been stalled for the moment due to disagreements around valuation and where the central bank should be based.

Saudi Arabia (KSA) weights 49% of the total economy, for 60% of the population. Whilst the United Arabic Emirates (UAE) have been the main growth engine over the last 15 years, KSA is slowly coming into a pole position, thanks to the *Vision 2030* plan, launched in 2016, by the Crown Prince Mohammed bin Salman. Vision 2030's main purpose is to reduce KSA's dependence on oil and gas by diversifying its economy, and developing public service sectors such as health, education, infrastructure, and recreation and tourism. Back in 2017, the Crown Prince pledged for a moderate Saudi Arabia: *"...we want to go back to what we were before 1979: a moderate Islam that is open to all religions and to the world and to traditions and people."*

Culture

It is a pleonasm to state that the Arabic culture dominates the region. However, the most dynamic country, the UAE, has widely opened to different countries. Emiratis weight only 11% of the population, whilst Hindis represent 38%. Dubai, in particular, is a place where the Middle Eastern normal rules don't really apply. It is a sort of an island, on which anyone is welcome as long as they contribute to wealth creation.

Where to Go?

Most dynamic market and most open to the world, the UAE would be my first recommendation as a first base. It has cemented its reputation as the regional and international gateway. You are an 8-hour flight away from 2/3 of the world's population—Asia, Russia, Europe, and Africa—and well connected to emerging markets. Through its large selection of Free Zones, you can benefit from 100% ownership, with no restrictions on funds repatriation, full exemption from corporate and personal income tax, and full exemption of import/export duties, as long you don't sell B-to-C into the UAE. The country is very stable and truly business culture driven. However, I would highly recommend you establish yourself through a legal counselling firm that can, almost by hand holding, take you through the process of company incorporation and individual 'Emiratisation' of your director (or yourself). This legal partner must also support you through your annual obligations. I was fortunate enough to work with one who has been flawless during my mandate, and I am happy to give you a personal recommendation.

Until KSA's *Vision 2030* is properly rolled out, the UAE remains my number 1 recommendation for a GCC Hub.

4. North America

The US-Mexico-Canada agreement (USMCA) is also commonly called NAFTA 2.0 since it is a renegotiation of the North American Free Trade Agreement (NAFTA), which was originally signed in 1994.

Foundation: 2020	Members: 3
Population: 490 mio	GDP: $24.8 trillion
Area: 21.5 mio km²	GDP/capita: $54,700

Source: The Economist – 2020 World in figures

Economic

The original NAFTA promoted the free movement of goods, services, and capital, but excluded the free movement of labour. The exchange between US and Canada became completely free, whilst keeping few exceptions where Mexico still had tariffs. The USMCA reformed few provisions, and increased barriers for goods, mainly in automotive and dairy. Economic experts and the International Monetary Fund (IMF) expect those modifications to have very little impact on the economy and the GDP of the three nations.

Culture

Historically, North America is a block made by immigrants; the two world wars have only reinforced this trend. So it will be little surprise to you that you can find any culture or foreign community across the continent: Europeans in the Northeast US; French community in Montreal and Quebec; Asian on the West coast, from San Francisco to Vancouver. However, the first culture is business, and its first symbol is $.

Where to Go?

From a sales perspective, the USA, across most industries, is organised through "reps" (sales representatives). Whether small organisations or individuals, they are signed up by manufacturers and paid via commissions. In most of the cases, the goods flow directly from the manufacturer to the reps' customers. This means you will need a regional logistic platform from which you can dispatch across the 3 countries. Considering the size of the market, a foreign SME may find it very difficult to finance an appropriately sized operation. An option could be to enter an association with a local partner, under either a distribution agreement or even a joint venture.

5. South America

Mercosur is the South American trade block established in 1991. As of 2020, it has 5 full members: Argentina, Brazil, Uruguay, Paraguay, and Venezuela. The latter has been suspended since late 2016, for breaching the democratic order and not complying with Mercosur agreements. The block also includes 7 associate members: Bolivia, Chile, Colombia, Ecuador, Guyana, Peru, and Suriname.

Foundation: 1991 **Population:** 300 mio **Area:** 295 mio km²	**Members:** 4 (+1 suspended) + 7 associates **GDP:** $4.6 trillion **GDP/capita:** $19,538

Source: The Economist – 2020 World in figures

Economic

Mercosur promotes free movement of goods, capital, and labour between its members. Its performance has lately reached a GDP of $4.6 trillion, positioning the block to the 5th economy of the world. Over the last 14 years, Mercosur has signed free trade agreements with Japan, Israel, Lebanon, and the European Union. The Common Market Council and Common Market Group are respectively the highest authority and the executive body to conduct and implement policy decided in the Mercosur Parliament (ParlaSur).

Culture

As former Portuguese and Spanish colonies, the culture remains very Latino across the region. You will find business people speaking English (or Dutch), but Portuguese and Spanish prevails.

Where to Go?

The region has 2 highly urbanised and centralised megapolis: Sao Paulo in Brazil (22 mio inhabitants), and Buenos Aires in Argentina (16 mio inhabitants), both on the Atlantic side. Secondary cities would be Montevideo (Uruguay), Caracas (Venezuela) in the north, and Rio de Janeiro (Brazil). I would recommend you aim for the 2 biggest cities, if your activity is not in farming or the natural resource sector.

6. Asia-Pacific

The Association of South Eastern Asia Nations (ASEAN) was originally composed because of a common fear of communism, by Indonesia, Malaysia, Philippines, Singapore, and Thailand. Over the years, they were joined by Brunei, Vietnam, Laos, Myanmar, and Cambodia.

Foundation: 1967 **Population:** 660 mio **Area:** 4.5 mio km²	**Members:** 10 **GDP:** $3.3 trillion **GDP/capita:** $5,122

Source: The Economist – 2020 World in figures

Economic

The ASEAN Free Trade Agreement (AFTA), signed in 1992, was a free trade agreement in name only. It created an area where state members were free to apply reduced tariffs (between 0 and 5%), under the so-called Common Effective Preferential Tariff (CEPT). Since 2015, ASEAN intends to implement a proper single market involving the free movement of goods, services, capital, and labour, but the project remains a 'work in progress,' with the ambitious goal to deliver in 2025.

ASEAN is also part of the Asia Pacific Economic Council (APEC), involving another 11 states, amongst which you find China, USA, Canada, Japan, and Australia. APEC's purpose is to facilitate exchanges between members, and contribute to their economic growth.

ASEAN is also part of the Pacific Economic Cooperation Council (PECC), a network of countries to promote cooperation across the region.

Culture

Taking aside China, South Eastern Asia is a very fragmented area, where many small countries and economies constitute a large patchwork of diverse languages and currencies. Everything works the Asian way or the ASEAN Way: Respect of cultural norms, compromise, consensus, and consultation are the informal decision making process. Conflicts are seen as weaknesses and must be avoided, or you risk losing face. This can lead to a piling up of agreements, councils, and associations, which can be difficult to read through, even for economic and political experts.

Where to Go?

As you will understand, with all the economic and political agreements still in progress, and their benefits unknown, it makes it difficult to make a decision based on single market access. Since post-WWII, the most common entry point to Asia was Hong Kong: *London in Asia* with all its British finesse, tradition, and well-known environment. Over the last 16 years, whilst using the former British colony as my home when in Asia, I could see the slow but certain reduction of British influence. Sadly, this trend has been accelerating over the last few years. You may find a logical and very commonly used alternative to HK by flying 4 hours southwest to Singapore. Singapore offers similar benefits to HK, with an overall English speaking population, no tax on capital gains or inheritance, and gives you access to the future ASEAN single market.

Chapter VI

Build Global Teams

1. Culture – Values – Mission – Purpose

Your role as a CEO is to lead from the inside out, and to create and guard a space for others to shine. Instead of creating a climate of fear, and leading in a command and control style, you create a purpose-driven culture, which encourages open communication and empowers your people to access their full potential.

Once, I was told a true leader can be compared to a conductor of an orchestra: You develop a vision, orchestrate people around a common purpose, and create the space in which all your teams can flourish and improve their skills at the service of the greater good of your company.

In this chapter, we will find how culturally different people can be; and where most of the people hire likeminded people, you can create global teams with exponential talents. Your blend of Western, Asian, or Middle Eastern culture, together, will make your organisation a success, whilst driving its value higher and faster than any of your competitors. How will you achieve this?

Culture

No nationality or culture is greater than the company's is. Your culture, your values, your purpose, and your mission will prevail any nationality or culture. Culture is usually built from the top; you as a leader have to set the example.

Values

I often hear SME CEOs commenting that values, missions, and purpose is a communication gadget gimmick for large multinationals: They are written in glossy annual reports and written on the wall of luxury head offices without anyone noticing. They could not be more wrong.

Closely linked to your brand, values are a few single words that describe your company, your offer, and your teams in the best possible way. Every employee should be able to recognise himself in the 3 to 5 words describing what your company stands for. Also, when you recruit, you or any of your managers can ask yourselves which candidates fit the best to your values!

There are different ways in which corporate values can be picked. One of them is that you decide and communicate them top down; another one is to benchmark your competitors or companies you admire. Another way is to federate your teams; I mean, literally, every employee, and invite them all to give their manager (anonymously or not) 3 words or expressions that they can relate the company and their colleagues to. Once you receive all the feedback, you can allocate it to around 3 to 5 key words that will eventually become your core values. Introduce and discuss them in your boardroom, and eventually organise a formal presentation to your employees, who will then be fully part of it. Once adopted, those values should be etched in stone and be communicated widely, internally as well as externally. When I did this exercise, I was surprised how quickly our teams identified around them, and how fast managers assessed new incomers on how well they fit with us.

Mission/Purpose

Share the vision and strategy you have designed in the previous chapter. People feel part of a shared mission: This then becomes a shared common purpose. It makes work engaging and exciting, and drives people to go the extra mile without noticing. This is an additional asset to attract younger generations, who are more driven by contributing to a shared mission rather than securing a lifetime career.

Now that you have defined your culture and shared your purpose, everyone on board can bring their contribution to achieve the common goals. You can, from there, build up a culture of winners and achievers, where back seat drivers will naturally be rejected, should you get the wrong people on board.

Accountability

Being held accountable can feel stressful for people, whilst it actually gives a sense of purpose and significance. By holding someone accountable, you communicate that you care about them. For example, when you tell your children that you expect them to bring home good grades, you are in fact telling them about your awareness of how intelligent they are, and that you only want them to succeed. This is also true in companies: When holding people accountable to deliver ambitious goals, you actually tell them that you value their contribution and that it does matter to their teams, your company, and you.

2. Motivate the Organisation

As a self-made person, you may find yourself managing from too close: Nothing is more demotivating or more value destructive than micro-management. For building and managing global teams, you will have to create a culture of entrepreneurship, in which everyone can make as many mistakes as they want, as long they learn from it (but do not repeat it over and over again). Your team will need to own their projects, and learn to live, act, and make their decisions with the consequences of successes and failures. It is also key that you make them comfortable to ask for help, without having them feel ashamed or inferior. This is particularly true in some cultures where people are supposed to know everything, and where asking for help can be considered as weakness. (See Chapter VII)

As a top university graduate, from which you will have built a solid career in a strategy consulting or audit firm, you may find yourself managing from too far. SME teams like to see their CEO involved, getting his hands dirty in all sort of operational issues: key account management, supplier chasing, quality issues, or even work on a production line! They will then respect their CEO as one of them, who can lead by example and doesn't refuse any duty he would ask from his staff. As an example, I have seen CEOs and chairmen spending their weekends manufacturing items to help ramp up volumes in a peak month! How can a production operator ever forget that his major shareholder has been working next to him, on a shift, manufacturing the same product he/she does, just to help them to come out of a bottleneck?

When you build up teams from dozens of different nationalities and cultures, it is your responsibility as a CEO to make sure they all merge and work in perfect harmony. One of the risks you will face is to see a development of small clans or clubs, such as the "German corner" or the "French club," close to the coffee machine. Tensions can arise if, in an open space, you have a few people talking in their native language, surrounded by others who don't understand a word. Not only is this rude, but it is also counterproductive and distractive. This is a NO-GO: It's your manager's and, ultimately, your direct responsibility to kill this off as it emerges: No nationality or culture is bigger than the company culture you (and your team) have established together, and you as the CEO are the ultimate guardian.

Instil a Value Creation Culture

When your teams ask for a spend approbation, I recommend you use the opportunity to turn it into a big lesson just by asking, 'What is the created value?' For example:

Your Sales & Marketing team wants to exhibit at a trade show:

- How much more business will this show generate?
- How much did it generate last time we exhibited?
- How long is the payback?

During that show, picking up the challenge, your teams will be in the booth and will look for a way to generate an additional sale to cover for it....and prove they were right.

Your Operations team wants to do a 10-day tour in Asia to visit suppliers and subcontractors:

*   How will you pay it back?
*   From where will you gain a price reduction during this trip?
*   Which new solution to reduce your operational costs will you find during this trip?

During either event, the payback will remain a recurring topic of amusement. If you achieve it, celebrate it; if you don't, just accept the learned lessons. The ultimate bonus of this exercise is that you educate your teams to think as entrepreneurs, and any individual involved will start thinking in value creation and payback times.

Mentoring and Coaching

Part of your managers' and your own job is to mentor and coach your teams to succeed. I find it more efficient and natural when the mentoring process is initiated by the subordinate. Your team member is hungry to learn, asks to go on a course, or seeks your recommendation for a book? Feed him, as much as you can. I am a big believer in buying proactive books for people, to support a message or help them in their lives. Sometimes people buy in, and sometimes they don't even open the book; it is their individual choice. Too often, I hear about managers who force mentoring and coaching on their teams—forcing them to take a course, or ordering them to read books, and asking for a written book review. Your teams are professional adults, household runners, parents, and grandparents. Treating them like pupils doesn't work and will backfire on you. The question you can ask yourself is, what is most important for you—shaping individuals to your image, or supporting them to achieve the company goals in their own way?

Virtual Teams

Since Covid-19, we hear how great virtual teams are, how easy and comfortable it is to work from home, and we wonder why we haven't done it earlier. This obviously works well for established teams that have been built, and have a history and existing relations, but how would this work for teams to be built? How can you integrate a newcomer? How will he/she learn and live through your values and company culture? How could you as an incoming CEO drive change?

3. Get the Right People In...

Now that you have defined your culture, your objectives, and what you stand for as an organisation, you must build your team. Where do you start?

Who Are Your Assets?

First of all, you should start reviewing your human capital, and assess how much you can build on them. By now, everyone in your company should have understood, accepted, or at least been made aware of what the company wants to stand for, and what the 5-year vision is, so that everyone can, in an informal discussion, bring their thoughts and goodwill, and explain how they will contribute to the project.

By experience, you will find that 10% of your staff were waiting for such a visionary project, can't wait to get started, and will storm your office with new ideas and quick changes to make the company better short term. Those individuals are the pillars of your strategy, and of the company you want to build; keeping a close connection with them will not only emulate motivation between you and them, but it will also spread around the organisation.

Eighty percent of your staff will keep doing their job in the same way and in the same dynamic, because 'this is how we have always done it.' They are the people who wait and see: Is this glorious project only a shooting star? How long will it last before it's completely forgotten? If you are a CEO who has been recently appointed by shareholders to drive change, those 80% may even wonder how long you will last before the next CEO comes in with another shooting star vision and project. To make it short, those 80% sit on the fence and wait for things to happen, and will eventually follow the movement of the majority.

Sadly, you shall find the last 10% to be rather against you than behind you. Their reasons and motivations can be very diverse: They don't like your face, your accent, or the colour of your tie. They don't believe in your project and have no will to be part of it. Some of them may leave; others will wait for you to fall, and may even help you to fall. Those last 10% will be value destroyers, and will be a bad influence on the 80%. The next section explains how to manage them.

A cultural change is heavy enough; if you try to carry it out on your own, you may sink. The key is to use your 10% convinced staff to relay and amplify the dynamic and changing atmosphere, and it will positively contaminate the 80% 'fence-sitters.' Very much like in a sport team, where the manager needs his dressing room leaders to convey his ideas, you need your leaders to transmit yours.

Creating a culture of winning performance has to start from the top of the company, down to the last employee. Values have to be adopted, believed in, and aspired by everyone, internally as well as externally.

Your Senior Management Team

I cannot address the importance of your senior management team (SMT); the example starts in the boardroom. Your SMT, including your chairman, non-executive directors, and potential shareholders, must be your backup, as well as the relay of your changes, and fully aligned behind the project you have all committed to. If one team member is not, your engine is running with a missing valve. A common situation that I have seen and experienced in SMEs is often due to the size of your company: You can't afford a top management team since this would blow up your overhead and kill your profits. So it does take several years of hard work, from other team members and yourself, to compensate the missing valve until you reach the level where you can eventually afford to inboard high flyers. Once you have your full team on board, your results will be exponential, and you will wonder what could have happened if you'd had them a few years earlier! I can only recommend you get them on board as soon as you can afford them: Not only is it well invested money, but it also should be paid back within a year. If it isn't, you have the wrong addition to your team.

A solid management team should have the following directors reporting to you:

- Sales
- Finance & Infrastructure
- Operations
- Marketing & Commercial (can include New Product Development)

Your added cost for four directors (fully packaged) can reach £350k. Divide this by your gross margin, and it will tell you how much more sales you need to generate, or how much cost efficiencies you need to find, to at least break even.

Building a team and hiring people is always a sort of adventure and can stimulate some excitement, but adventures often come with their fair share of disappointments. You will increase your share of success by reducing the unknowns.

Deciding what you want, and writing a job description, is the easy part. A more difficult question to answer is, 'Who do YOU want?'

How many industries do you know that are not incestuous? Who hasn't seen industry tourists going from one competitor to another, especially in the sales function? What credibility would you give to a sales person telling you product A is so much better than B, whilst he was selling product B for years? I can only recommend you consider parallel or even completely different industries; your new recruit may take a bit longer to learn, but the contribution he can make from other industries will enrich your teams, company, and ultimately value.

Foreigners, Minority Ethnics, and Gender Equality

For becoming a global SME, you need to embrace diversity, and mix cultures, nationalities, languages, backgrounds, and gender. The value generated by a global team is difficult to describe. It will become a core part of your company culture; the newly created group dynamic will open minds on the world, and make you part of it.

I would also add a note on gender equality. Unfortunately, some industries are far too much gender polarised, and you will find it another way to enrich your company's value. One of my lifelong role models once said: *'If you are in a tough position, just get a smart woman on board, and she will figure it all out for you.'* In one of my recent jobs, I was very proud to leave a 50/50 gender-equal, direct report executive team, in a 90% male-dominated industry. You will find some women being excellent sales people, knowing their products, their competitors, and their customers better than their male colleagues. Why? Probably because they always had to prove they were better, and keep wanting to prove it daily.

As long as people fit the company culture and values, you should not care about their gender, culture, or industry experience. The era of colonialism is over; do not expect international success if you don't have diverse teams and don't master foreign languages. Never pretend: You will not be taken seriously.

Recruitment

Anyone who has dealt with headhunters, as a candidate or as a recruiter, will admit that the quality of the provided service 'varies,' and cost doesn't necessarily reflect value. For you, the SME CEO, I would recommend to identify a privately owned boutique recruiting firm (specialised or not), one on which you can rely and even establish a long-term relationship, ideally with the same consultant. First, he/she will know you as a person and as a manager, and hence what fits you best and what does not. Second, once he/she has found, for example, three possible team members, he/she will know exactly which one will fit in the company culture and work well with the other team members you have hired.

To reduce the risk of failure to a minimum level, some companies give the last few candidates a 'day in.' After having signed a non-disclosure agreement (NDA), candidates come in the company and are free to walk around, speak, and invite anyone in the company to an individual discussion, in a similar way an auditor would do. Later in the month, candidates are invited back to present to your SMT their diagnostic, action plan, and detailed first 100 days. There are several benefits to this process: First, it is irrelevant if you agree or disagree with their presentation, but it demonstrates their way of thinking. Second, should the candidate be appointed, he/she can hit the ground running almost immediately. Third, and most importantly, candidates will have worked with you and your teams outside a classic job interview mode, and will have a feeling for a future collaboration. Recruiting is like dating: Each party chose each other...or not!

Unfortunately, recruitment mistakes still do happen. One of the reasons is because you and I believe everyone else knows what we know. In one of my roles, I was part of the executive team of a €100m division, and we all realised that our newly appointed divisional managing director had no clue how a P&L works, and had never heard of depreciation/amortization. Embarrassing. You may think that such things only happen in multinationals, where wrong people in the wrong position just get 'promoted internally' to a different position or division. This can happen to you! More recently, I appointed a company accountant, in line to become our next finance director, and discovered (too late) that this person didn't know that a balance sheet has to balance! A SME cannot afford to pay for incompetence. In recruitment, there is always a 50/50 chance to get it right. And this is fine, as long you correct it when you are on the wrong side of the 50%— which leads us to the next section.

4. Get the Wrong People Out...

Years ago, I was told a story that occurred in the late 90s, in a very traditional family-owned SME in Italy, in a village east of Bergamo:

The scene takes place in an atmosphere like 'The Godfather': old-fashioned boardroom, wooden walls, wooden carpets, and paintings of the company's passed founder and following generations. In the middle of the room, you could find a massive oval oak table; and in front of each chair, there was a pure leather desk pad embroidered with the company's logo, with a company notepad and pencil, accompanied by a bottle of water and a glass for each participant. In the middle of the table stood a smiling stuffed monkey with cymbals in both hands. The occasion was one of the three annual meetings: a global business review, inviting every country's manager from across the globe. Twelve people were sitting around the table, reporting one by one, over the 3 days, how their territories were performing. It was only at the end of day 3—after the wrap-up—that the North American country manager (an American) dared to ask what the purpose of the stuffed monkey was. The company owner raised his eyes to the sky and said: 'Thank God, someone dares to say something.' He then explained that this was a major lesson he wanted every manager to take back to his local teams: 'During 3 days, all of you knew that this monkey wasn't at his place, didn't fit in this room, and didn't bring any value to the discussions. Even worse, it did generate a bit of distraction, but NOBODY talked about it. This is how teams work; we all have our monkeys in our teams, and I do want you to talk about it, encourage your teams to talk about it, and fix the problem.'

This real story demonstrates how we as humans operate: We all know that James from accounts is useless, or that Ingrid from the sales team doesn't pull her weight; but since they have been here forever, and we do like them as individuals, we look away and accept them as dead wood that we have to carry with us. This is not acceptable for any team or organisation that strives for performance and high achievements: Not only do you pay someone who doesn't do their job, and underperforms, but you demotivate the big contributors by letting a bad example go untouched. Those individuals may even be on the same company performance bonus scheme and make the same bonus as devoted performers! How demotivating is that?

Underperformance Is Contagious

A few years ago, I sat in a sales meeting, in an ambitious SME whose goal was to double revenue over the next 5 years. Every regional sales manager reported his previous month's activities, how much he would fall short from achieving his monthly targets, and explained why he would not deliver. When asked how many customer visits he had made the previous month, he proudly said "12!" Indeed, 12 was his number of visits the previous month, as well as his average over the last 10 months. Considering that the industry's average number of visits was 6 to 8 per day, he was asked why there were so few; to which he replied that he would lose in quality if he was stretched to do more. Satisfied with this explanation, the sales director moved to the next regional sales manager. Guess how many visits the second regional sales manager reported? Twelve! How many visits did the third regional manager report? Twelve again!

This demonstrates how fast a team can become complaisant or even rotten. A hidden collusion between the existing underperformers lowers the standards and delivers underperformances after underperformances. This gets even worse: Imagine that you inject new blood to boost morale and impulse a dynamic in your sales effort. What will happen to your new addition after being 6 months in? He/she will report 12 visits per month!

You can add as many resources as you like, but if you keep looking away from the rotten apples, they will always contaminate others and destroy value.

Underperformance is like a virus: If not eradicated, it will spread around and become the new standard without anyone noticing it!

Trust Your Gut Feeling and Act Without Fear

A common factor in SME poor performers is that they survive because 'they have always been there.' After a while, they get bolder and bolder; they don't even hide anymore, and they feel bulletproof. You find them watching TV on their laptops, or maximising their 'off-sick days' allowance: becoming sick on Fridays and Mondays, but when back on Tuesdays, they make sure everyone knows what a fantastic weekend they had! Despite everyone knowing, the management, or you as CEO, don't pull the trigger. Why? Do you worry about the internal repercussions and what people will say? How will it affect morale and productivity? Can this backfire? Trust your gut feeling and decide based on the company values. My personal experiences have demonstrated that in 99% of such situations, your teams do come back to you with the same question: 'What took you so long?'

Conflict Management

In a winning organisation, you will find passionate people, but as driven and dedicated as your teams are, you will always face conflict-of-interest situations. This happened to me years ago, when I was an overconfident (!?) sales director with a slice of an impetuous character: I had a fallout with a colleague, and the incident became apparent in the boardroom, involving our CEO. After the meeting, the CEO let me indirectly know that I should make peace with my colleague since we were both creating value for the company, and if we couldn't find our way to each other, we would both be gone! I refused, drove home, and convinced myself that I was unreplaceable because I was creating more value than my counterpart. The next morning, I arrived very early and, whilst leaving my car, I was called up by my CEO, who had his morning cigarette in front of his office. He always reminded me of John Wayne sitting outside his sheriff office:

'Sandy, I need to tell you something...'

- 'Yes, Larry. I am listening!'
- 'In my f***ing entire career, only once I had someone who was UNREPLACEABLE. You understand? Only ONCE.' He then threw away his cigarette stub and added: 'But I can't remember his name!'

Can you guess what happened next? My counterpart and I made peace.

When conflicts happen, they bring their positives if driven by genuine reasons, so you should accept and even favour the discussion for the greater good of the company. However, you ought to be careful not to be dragged into a wrong-or-right debate. If the involved parties are smart, they will figure it out between them, even if they are your direct reports.

Family Links

A very common issue in SMEs, especially if family-owned, is 'the monkey on the table': a family member or a very long servant of the owner—someone who has 'always been there.' Once, I had a factory manager who was part of the company since its inception 35 years earlier, and he was a poor performer. He had grown through the ranks, not for his performances or know-how, but only through who he actually knew. When I addressed the issues to the owner, I was told: 'He has always been here; he lives on site, looks after my house when I am away, and washes my car every Sunday morning, so he is here to stay until he re-tires.

So, if you are an owner, please keep in mind that loyalty is re-spectable, but it should not give a lifetime pass to underperformance.

If you are an employed CEO or minority shareholder, you are left with the option to reposition him into a role where he could potentially generate additional value (at least he stops destructing value). This gives you an open position to hire a talented, driven achiever, who actually does fit with your culture and values. You still have to accept that the salary for your 'monkey on the table' weights in your P&L, year after year.

The other option you have is to leave; there is no way an employed CEO will win a fight against family links. The core message here is as difficult and uncomfortable as the position might be: **Do not look away, and do address the issue** with the owning family, because the situation will not get better, and the monkeys will not go away. Why would they?

Happy Endings

Fortunately, not every underperformer has to leave the organisation, and I am a great believer in supporting people going through a rough time. Albeit you are not a priest or a social aider, it's part of your role to help people and guide them to success. We all live in a real world, where personal issues do arise and sadly influence individual performances. Sometimes simple solutions can be found in a one-to-one conversation with your team member: salary advance to fix an unexpected cash shortage, temporarily accommodating working hours for personal issues, or just by giving time to go through a difficult emotional time. Once your colleague is over the situation, he/she will be grateful for your support and will perform again and show loyalty to the company (and to you). You may even see an unusual overperformance to pay you back! Of course, such situations are easier to apprehend once the relation is established: You are more inclined to listen to a value generator who breaks down, rather than a newcomer who has never performed. It's vital to give time to newcomers too, and to avoid becoming a hire/fire company. It is your role, as a CEO, to make sure your teams maintain a clear line between supporting and being blinded.

In conclusion, you should always be supportive and listen to issues happening in everyone's real lives. You only need to be mindful not to start justifying the unjustifiable, or soon you (and your leadership team) will be excusing the inexcusable! This is a difficult balance to maintain and is all part of the joy of management.

5. Attract Talents...and Retain Them

Your Pyramid of Age Is a Value Driver Too!

Now that you have the right people in and the wrong people out, you will need to keep injecting new blood and additional energy. You need to keep in mind that your pyramid of age does impact the value of your company. A few years ago, my team and I were on an acquisition path, and we considered a 30-person company, whose employees' average age was 63 years! By the time we would have sealed the deal and started the post-acquisition work, most of them would have retired, and we would have lost a high value of knowledge and experience, basically buying an empty shell.

Your Competitive Advantage in the Job Market

As a SME CEO, you are well aware of the difficulty of attracting talents, especially younger ones. Your major competitors in the job market have much more competitive advantages: higher salaries, and larger benefits, such as private health, generous pension schemes, discount rates at groceries stores, design shops, or even gym clubs, all enclosed under a big, shiny, and well-known brand.

Once more, it demonstrates how much of an asset your brand is. It might be less known than a stock listed name, but this doesn't mean you can't valorise it in the eyes of future (and existing) employees. Your brand will shine through your products and services, but also via the values and purpose you have chosen. Luckily, younger generations are less driven by finding a secure lifetime career, and are more attracted to contributing to a common mission: a purpose to make tomorrow's world—their world—a better place to live. Never underestimate the power of meaningfulness; it creates excitement and engagement on a daily basis, to contribute to the greater good of the world.

For more senior profiles, I would encourage you to consider people without a job. Having been on both sides of the table, I can guarantee you that by giving a job to a jobless person, it buys you loyalty and overperformance, even more so if this person has been made redundant unfairly. This is also a differentiation factor from multinationals, who too often have the postulate: 'If out of a job, this candidate is not good enough for us!' If he fits your values and mission, what do you have to lose? Give him/her a chance to convince you.

Improve the Value of Your People

Younger generations who buy into your values and mission, will be empowered and take ownership of their work as they never would in a multinational. I would highly recommend you hire a few in apprenticeship schemes; in some countries, you can find ratios of 5 weeks in the company, for 1 week in school! If managed well, you have a homemade and educated talent for the next 5 to 7 years.

Another way to increase your company's and your people's value is to train them professionally. Most countries give you generous financial help (grants, tax reductions, etc.) for enrolling your team members in a professional program. You, as a company, should be proactive and offer it to people asking for it. It demonstrates a solid motivation to make themselves better professionals and to bring a larger contribution to your business. Forcing them is counterproductive.

Phantom Share Scheme

A much-underutilised way in SMEs to retain key contributors and high flyers, is by offering them equity in the company. Any of you who have dealt with SME shareholders, knows how sensitive such a discussion can be, and how long it can drag on.

The solution is a phantom share plan: It gives selected employees many of the benefits of shares ownership without actually giving them any company shares, so existing shareholders are not diluted. You can decide if those phantom shares pay dividends (taxed as ordinary income rather than capital gains), or if you link them to a potential company exit.

It increases the employee's ownership feeling and will give an additional drive to increase the company value since he will be paid a share of the sales price once you finalise your exit transaction. You can sell it as a sort of lottery ticket, with an increased chance of winning. However, my experience has demonstrated that such schemes should be limited in time; if people cannot see the horizon of the exit process (basically the date of the lottery draw), they can disengage and leave the company (and their phantom shares) anyway!

You will find examples of such schemes on the book's website.

Chapter VII

Manage Global Teams

n this chapter, we will review a selection of 'stereotypes' per culture. You will first find France, Germany, and the United Kingdom, since those 3 represent 40% of the geographical Europe population. We will then review USA, Middle East, and Asia. The principle of stereotypes is to give you an understanding of who acts how, and why, and can give you guidance on how to manage a particular profile. Those lines should not be taken religiously, nor to the dot, but only to reduce the amount of surprises when meeting a different culture.

1. France

The French have a very ambiguous relation to authority. The most symbolic example is during presidential elections: For the first 6 months, the elected president is seen as the saver and can walk on water; unfortunately, after 6 months, the revolutionary spirit surfaces again, and the hero becomes zero and should have his head cut off.

Savoir-vivre

The French give a lot of importance to etiquette and protocols, and expect respect for titles, and for rules of hierarchies and precedence. Traditionally, they are rarely called by their first names, and *Monsieur* and *Madame,* before the surname, is a must in every professional discussion. However, first names are becoming common practice for younger generations or in Anglo-Saxon multinational companies. The handshake is a ritual at the beginning and the end of any meeting. In the Southeast of France, it is very common to see a double or triple cheek kiss between colleagues. The correct use of the language matters a lot; how you speak and write is a sign of a good education.

Communication

Formalism and rituals protect individual autonomy. Relations that are too cordial or too familiar in the workplace can be seen as a means of manipulation of the employee, or subordination of his interests to those of the company.

The French rate highly the quality of written communication, form and presentation, of professional teams: complexity of polite formulas in letters, and proper use of the French language (vocabulary, grammar...).

The French rarely approach a subject directly: They beat around the bush, ask to be understood half-heartedly, and need to create a climate of trust and to know the person well before getting to the point.

They are fond of rhetoric, logic, and good reasoning, and enjoy arguments and never shy away from a lively debate. The French negotiator often relies more on concepts than on facts or figures. He is generally firm, coming across as intransigent, and tries to come to a "take it or leave it" offer. However, the French are not natural negotiators, in commercial or social fields. They don't really believe in win-win situations, and are more on the path of: *'If you win, I lose.'* This partly explains the painful strikes and unsuccessful negotiations with trade unionists.

Foreign Languages

Historically, the French were (with the British) amongst the Europeans who spoke the least foreign languages; probably a heritage of the time of greatness when the French language and culture was at the heart of diplomatic and intellectual Europe. Nowadays, 60% of the people aged 25–64, report speaking one or more foreign languages *(Source: Eurostat).*

Meetings

The French don't have a culture of teamwork: Individualism predominates, and relations between individuals or groups are based on independence more than on cooperation.

The meetings are very formal, are often linked to a strong hierarchical presence, and have everything structured and framed (very precise agenda, agreed intervention...). Any question is seen as an attack or a challenge. They are not looking for exchange and consensus, but for information.

Being anarchic, the absence of hierarchy leads to meetings that can easily come to a 'laissez-faire attitude': disrespect of the agenda, verbal jousts, digressions, expression of ideas in all directions, absence of production, and synthesis or consensus. The purpose of such meetings is not to fix the problem or make a decision, but rather to exchange information on mutual positions, around a given situation, problem, or issue.

Punctuality is key. Arriving later than 10 minutes is a clear lack of respect—if you believe you won't make it on time, you should contact the host and explain why you are going to be late. If you are in the Paris area, distances are never calculated in kilometres but in hours. Try to organise your meetings around traffic peak times.

Leadership

The traditional model of centralised authority is bureaucratic and autocratic: Authority is based on the status and technical competence, and so you find management by decree, by top executive, far away from the field.

The French have a fundamental ambivalence in relation to authority: One side shows much respect for hierarchy, submission, and deference; whilst the other side stays away from authority and aspires to independence.

Time Management

The French are intellectually monochronic (one thing at a time) but actually behave as polychronic (absence or non-respect of the plan; several activities to be carried out simultaneously), which doesn't give you a nice result. They are not good in terms of deadlines or appointments, and "emergencies" frequently take over the schedule. Punctuality depends on social circumstances and the importance of the person waiting.

Business meals are important and allow you to get to know each other in a favourable context. The average length of a business meal is 193 minutes in France, compared to 64 minutes in the

United States! You can still find a few industry sectors where it is very common to spend the day in an expensive restaurant's private room, from 11am till very late.

The French work until 7 or 8pm (especially in Paris). This can be attributed to either poor organisation or the weight of the hierarchical model: Being present late and not counting your hours is well seen by your hierarchy. The centralisation of the system does considerably increase the workload as you move up the ladder. Significant lunch breaks also shift the workday.

Organisation

The medium and long-term strategy planning is weak.

The too-long hierarchical lines leave little autonomy to the different management levels.

Narrow specialisation leads to much compartmentalisation, giving everyone the possibility to be his own cook in his own kitchen. This generates and cultivates a clan spirit, with potential rivalry in the organisation.

The French can't deny the importance of formalism related to organisational structures (organisation chart) and authority (respect for the hierarchical channel), but there is a lack of frequency of formalization of work rules (function and procedure). Functions are not defined with precision or just defined by a list of tasks, and are rarely defined in terms of objectives. Delegation is either micromanagement or very broad: The control is often seen as an interference and a lack of confidence towards an employee.

2. Germany

In uncertain times, populations look to their glorious pasts. Germany doesn't have one: After the Prussian Empire, the Weimar Republic, and the Third Reich, Germany had what they call "**Year 0,**" in 1945. Their principle is to focus on methodology and processes, and never to derogate.

Savoir-vivre

The formalism and respect for etiquette expects you to address someone by calling him/her Herr, Frau, or Fraulein, followed by his/her surname, or title and surname. Only younger and close colleagues will call each other by their first names, but not in an official meeting. The polite plural 'Sie' is largely predominant over the singular 'Du,' expressing great friendship or closeness. There is wide use of the titles Herr Doctor and Herr Professor: anyone who has completed a university degree in law, medicine, or economics, is called a doctor.

When people meet, a firm handshake is exchanged, although less frequently than in France.

Communication

The predominance of explicit communication makes it easy for foreigners: It results in the search of clear speaking, and straight to the point, direct, and frank messages. A German says what he thinks, even if it is not always pleasant. Likewise, an oral presentation in German will be concrete, logical, structured, and factual, with references and figures.

Germans keep their distance, and separate their private and professional spheres. To work together, they believe that people do not have to know each other in depth, or develop a relationship of friendship, but that the main thing is to build an agreement or modalities of cooperation on a technical and professional basis.

Thus, Germans can feel uncomfortable if asked for news of their families, or if invited to a business meal to get acquainted, but will be eager for details on a product or a process.

The Germans are tough negotiators: They are well prepared, express their offer clearly and firmly, and concede little.

Foreign Languages

Germans have ramped up their foreign language skills since the late 90s: 78% of the people, aged 25–64, report speaking one or more foreign languages *(Source: Eurostat).*

Meetings

Meetings are usually scheduled well in advance, have a clear agenda, and are debriefed. Their purpose is functions of coordination, mutual information, and ratification of decisions already made, more so than problem solving and decision making.

The meeting leader and group members stick to the agenda and the scheduled meeting time, and eliminate any other business. The participants prepare, argue, and justify their intervention, which avoids a priori judgments and premature conclusions. Discussions are frank, open, and can be vehement.

Leadership

There is respect towards authority, and orders are obeyed; subordinates do not criticise, and contradict their leader very rarely. The importance given to the hierarchical position, while remaining strong, has declined however, since World War II.

The consultation process, and search for consensus through discussion in the decision making process, can be seen as slow, but the implementation of the decision is then faster. Contrary to stereotypes, the German management style is not authoritarian. Of course, the German companies show a deep respect for hierarchy and centralised control methods. But at the same time, the number of hierarchical levels and the supervision rate are shorter and easier than in France; the delegations and the autonomy of employees are more widely developed.

Time Management

Time is a rare resource; everything has to be programmed, optimised, and compartmentalised.

Catch-ups and working sessions are kept brief: You stay in the frame and objectives, and you avoid off-topics. External disturbances are refused (phone, texts, visits, various requests).

Germans are obsessed with punctuality and accuracy, and have rigorous respect for timelines and deadlines.

The sense of the long term and the investment manifests itself in different areas: business strategy, work relationship, and decision making. This is even more recognisable in family-owned businesses, where the purpose is to keep improving the company for future generations.

Organisation

Germans love order, planning, rigor, discipline, methods, reliability, precision, and perfection. They hate waste, improvisation, blurring, uncertainty, and unconsidered action. Changing your plans, going back on a previously made decision, not respecting a procedure or a deadline, or not following an action taken, are unacceptable and are qualified as an irresponsible behaviour.

Lenin once said: "When the Germans want to storm a station platform, they first validate their tickets so that everything is in order!"

Rules and procedures, including detailed job specifications, are a must; which without, a German organisation would not start to operate.

Delegation is commonly used; they are clear, precise, and mostly written.

3. United Kingdom

The country is in search of its identity, which it has lost since the loss of the Victorian Empire, followed closely by the erosion of the Commonwealth. It's not uncommon to hear from Harrogate's pubs up into the highest political circles: 'We won the war; we beat the Germans!' Or, 'We are the British Empire!' This shows how far Brits must fetch back.

Oddly enough, European neighbours have a secret nostalgic love affair with what they remember as being so English: eccentricity, pragmatism, phlegmatism, and a unique sense of humour. Sadly, this has slightly vanned in the last few years, with the entire world wondering what actually happened to Great Britain.

Savoir-vivre

You must know the difference between England, Great Britain (which includes England, Scotland, and Wales), and the United Kingdom (which includes the three previous countries plus Northern Ireland). Never ask Republic of Ireland citizens why they are not part of the UK!

The ritual of greeting consists of throwing a "How do you do?" echoed by another "How do you do?" The British practice the handshake much less than continental Europeans: It is exchanged during a first meeting, and afterwards, only in great formal occasions or of official character. It is incorrect to address a person to whom one has not been introduced.

You can easily and quickly call someone by their first name, even if you have known them very recently. This is a very common practice during a first business meeting.

Always refer to the social position and honorary or hereditary titles, such as Lord or Sir, even if not mentioned when you get to know each other, nor written on the business card.

Bowler hats are out of fashion nowadays, but club ties are still a social symbol: a sign of recognition and belongingness to a school, a regiment, or a university association. You shall be laughed at if you wear such an affiliated tie without belonging to the group it represents.

Accent is also a criterion of social recognition. The correct accent, or the "Queen's English," is apparently the one of BBC speakers. As a foreigner, you will always be asked where you are from, and almost straight after your introduction.

Communication

There is cultural and historical predominance of oral over writing. England has few written rules: no written constitution, no individual identity cards, and even the law is not written; hence, it is called 'common law.'

Pragmatism is key, and contrasts with abstraction, theorisation, and intellectualism.

Brits like indirect and allusive communication. A subject is not usually tackled head-on through figures, facts, and final judgment. They also generally avoid debates and contradictory confrontations; hence, the importance of humour, based on self-deprecation and understatements.

In general, they are reserved and have self-control, and show very little emotions whilst remaining very discreet about their private lives.

The British negotiator is concrete and cordial, but can sometimes come across as a little amateurish and insufficiently prepared; he responds with concessions and openings to the other party's proposals. You should not try to put too much pressure on them in order to bargain too much.

Foreign Languages

With little surprise, the United Kingdom comes last in the ranking of spoken foreign languages, with 35% of the age group, 25–64, speaking one or more foreign languages; which is just behind Romania, at 36% *(Source: Eurostat)*. Fortunately, since the entire business world speaks English, this doesn't prevent British SMEs from going global!

Meetings

Meetings and committees are important and very frequent, and they ease the life of the company. In general, they have a flexible agenda and favour abundance of informal exchanges over a cup of tea.

A specificity of business meetings in England is the dominance of football (soccer). I have been involved in meetings with customers or suppliers, where every participant introduced himself by referring to the club he supports. This is an ideal, quick icebreaker once you overcome the sarcasm or rivalry, especially if your counterpart's team didn't do well over the weekend.

Leadership

There is a large range of concepts about hierarchy and authority practices.

Brits like an unequal liberal model, which is a combination of an open model with being employee participation orientated, but is still marked by a social hierarchy coming from the establishment (Oxford/Cambridge).

The reference profile of the manager is more often the self-made man, who 'learned by doing' rather than the professional basing his authority on his competence and expertise.

Time Management

Punctuality is important. However, 10 minutes late is more easily tolerated than 10 minutes early. Appointments should always be scheduled in advance: 'Popping in' whilst on the road is considered as unprofessional.

Organisation

There is a clear predominance of opportunism over rigorous and systematic planning. Planning, when it exists, is essentially financial and is too often considered as an extension of the budgetary process. This can be associated with the mistrust of too much organisational formalism, which can be considered as useless bureaucracy.

Brits delegate easily, and like decentralised holding structures with weak central control. You can find many partitions between operational and functional, which often leads to insufficient control, and is more financial than managerial.

It's not unusual to find several shortcuts within the hierarchical line, based on personal relations. This syndrome is amplified in family-owned businesses, but is not specific to the United Kingdom.

4. USA

Savoir-vivre

'Good morning; my name is Bill J, sales director, and I make $150,000 per year!' Americans have become less and less formal, and never hide their drive to make money. America is the country of the dollar: Everything is linked to money. If asked about his company's size, a European will always first mention the number of employees (and the created jobs), whilst an American will tell you its revenues (and the generated profits). If you take aside the North Eastern states that are still under European cultural influence, you will rarely find a businessman wearing a suit and tie across the country. Chinos and shirts with company logo have become the standards.

Communication

Americans are very direct: A 'yes' means 'yes,' and a 'no' means 'no.' Discussions are always focused on facts and figures. Indirect approaches can be seen as indecision or, even worse, weakness. Money and money making is never a taboo.

You may find yourself surprised by what can be seen as an overplayed positivity, and the high use of 'Wonderful!' 'Amazing!' or the so overused, 'Awesome!' It actually does impact team spirit and performances positively, although it can feel odd to Europeans.

Foreign Languages

According to the Centre of Immigration Studies (CIS), 20% of the USA population speak at least one foreign language, which put into perspective, means 67 million people! This includes the native-born, and the legal and illegal immigrants. The number has more than doubled since 1990, and has almost tripled since 1980! With little surprise, the biggest part of these 67 million are located in the North Eastern and South Western states, plus Florida.

Meetings

A timed agenda is shared far ahead so that participants can prepare professionally. Video projectors are widely used since visuals permit to share information faster. There is little time left for questions. Should a non-agenda topic arise during the meeting, and there is need of further talks, a new meeting shall be organised. Physical or virtual meetings start and finish on time: Not doing so is considered a lack of respect for other participants' time (and money).

Leadership

An American CEO is expected to perform over 3 major fields: first, to manage his resources (human, technological, and financial) through budgets and objectives; second, to lead his team towards the common goal and make them all deliver their targets; and third, he is a coach who develops his teams and supports them in advancing their careers.

Hierarchy is much less formal than in Europe; everyone calls each other by their first name, and it's not unusual to see production operatives sitting next to the CEO during a lunch break. People like to learn from each other without any barriers; they all have a common religion: the dollar!

The American Leadership model is admired and respected across the globe. Americans know that, and they expect every businessperson to act as they do. The reality is a bit different and, although the world does adopt this model, it is highly adapted and influenced by local cultures.

Time Management

As mentioned in previous paragraphs, time is money! When people travel to visit customers, or commute to the office, most of them take planes and have to respect a schedule.

From a planning perspective, the American 'short-term' vision is a "quarter," in contrast to a year in Europe.

Organisation

Customer is king! American organisations are all 'customer focused,' as written in their most famous universities' books. In the last few years, we have seen organisations having a massive rise of 'vice-president of customer experience' positions. The experience doesn't only involve the products and their features, but also the full purchasing process, starting from product selection till after-sales service and guarantees!

The culture of the 'result' prevails, always. The equation is easy: Facts + Figures = Decision. Sometimes decisions can be made in a hasty way, but the result, and only the result, will prove the right from the wrong.

Despite corporate communication on *'we are a team'* and *'win as a team,'* America still has the culture of individualism over the collective. You will find this in business as much as in sports.

5. Gulf Countries

The countries from the Gulf region are the most conservative and traditional countries in the world. Whilst the Kingdom of Saudi Arabia (KSA) entangled itself in strong religion and sharia law in the late 70s, its neighbours opened slowly to Western cultures. The United Arabic Emirates (UAE), for example, has 88% immigrants as its total population. Over the last few years, KSA has launched their Vision 2030, pledging for a moderate Islam that is open to all religions, to the world, and to all traditions and people. The clear intent of 'Vision 2030' is to attract Western talents and cultures, to revive an economy that is over-reliant on oil and gas.

Savoir-vivre

You will be judged on your appearance, so men should wear a suit and tie, whilst women should dress conservatively and must keep their arms covered at any time. Business cards should ideally be printed in Arabic on one side, which should be presented first, at the beginning of the meeting. Ensure that you present and receive them with your right hand. The rule you should apply around the world is even truer here: Never discuss religion.

To ensure flawless cross-cultural relations, and avoid any faux pas, I would recommend you adopt a high degree of formality: showing respect and recognition to older people and those in senior positions.

The first name is the personal name followed by 'bin,' which means 'son of,' followed by the name of the father. This is then followed by the family name. For example, the current ruler of Dubai is Mohammed bin Rashid Al Maktoum—'Mohammed' being his first name, and then 'bin Rashid Al Maktoum' meaning 'the son of Rashid Al Maktoum.'

Communication

Business is very personal, where people buy from people, and it's almost impossible to conclude a deal without having met face-to-face and built a relationship.

Foreign Languages

The official language for all the Gulf countries is Arabic, although English is very commonly used. Foreign languages are pretty disparate, and depend on the distribution of population across the region: Persian, where you find expats from Iran; or Hindi, where you find people from India. With 38% of its population being Indian, Hindi is not very far behind Arabic as a major language.

Meetings

Appointments should be organised two weeks in advance, and I recommend you confirm a few days before. Very frequently, it can take place in a café or a hotel lounge.

Punctuality is important and expected from Western people, but not necessarily from your local contacts. As in many other countries, informal 'small talk' is common before addressing the agenda of the day. It remains an essential component in building relationships.

To the annoyance of Anglo-Saxon cultures, meetings can have several interruptions, such as loud mobile phone rings, which will, most of the time, be taken in front of you and make you a spectator of unprompted phone conversation. Also, some unrelated person could just join in the meeting and completely divert the conversation.

Leadership

The boss often holds a fairly paternalistic role. As such, it's not uncommon for conversations to move to more personal matters during discussions between a boss and a team member. This is especially true in family-owned companies, where the head of the family will most likely be the key decision maker. This is also true for any family-owned company in Europe.

Managers can question a decision that is made, whilst remaining careful not to lose face with the leader or owner. Employees never question decisions, and they execute what they are told to do. If in your Western style, you are a leader who values and promotes participation, you have to create a safe environment for people to start acting as such. This will be a change of the management process on its own.

Time Management

First of all, be aware that in Arabic countries, the working week runs from Sunday to Thursday—Friday and Saturday being the weekend.

Patience is a key element to succeed in the region. Everything takes longer than expected since the decision process can be unclear to external people, and meetings get interrupted. It is important not to show your frustrations. As a Western manager, establishing (gently and smoothly) a discipline of schedules, and a respect for deadlines, is culturally supported by the wave of Westernisation and globalisation hitting the region.

Organisation

Most organisations are very hierarchical, and organisation charts do exist, but the informal way is that everything goes and works around the patriarch. Decisions can be easily overturned.

Culturally, for Western people, the slow decision making and extremely bureaucratic processes can be infuriating. However, one should not rush the process and risk being seen as disrespectful. Also, as a manager, however right you may be, or how justifiable your decision might be, you may find yourself in the position of 'having to compromise,' if someone's face or dignity is at stake!

6. China

We have seen, in a previous chapter, how fragmented the Asia-Pacific region was with its patchwork of countries, languages, and cultures. Focusing on the Chinese management model should give you enough keys and concepts to sail through the entire region.

The Chinese pay particular attention to the administrative process, the government of people, and the modes of operation in international cooperation. Despite their respect for the hierarchy, they each see themselves as a centre of influence, around which the others gravitate. In addition, they consider it important to identify the key people in their entourage, to respect the primacy of the leader, and to get as close as possible to the person who holds the authority. Belonging to the group is vital. Finally, they believe that their efforts should focus on concrete and useful things.

Savoir-vivre

Relationship is everything: The group always prevails over the individual. Families and friendships are never broken.

Harmony is key: The Chinese hate conflict, and so you will always hear a 'Yes, Yes,' even if they don't mean it!

Social convention/worldly wisdom—how to deal with people and know your way around people—plays an important role in Chinese culture, both in personal life and at work.

There is a strong culture of gifts and gifting. As a business partner, gifts are generally linked to the historical culture of the province you find yourself in: silk, wooden articles, ceramic tea service set, or thoughtful gifts following festival themes like Mid-Autumn, Chinese New Year, etc. This should be of reasonable value considering the recent anti-corruption laws issued by the government.

Communication

It is recommended to keep repeating the same message several times to make sure you are understood. It is also crucial to ask for feedback. Feedback is not natural in Chinese culture, and the Chinese prefer to keep quiet rather than admit they didn't understand you.

Culturally, admitting a wrongdoing is a weakness, and people fear losing their authority or reputation, and being seen as incompetent. Teaching to share and learn from mistakes is a very slow 'work in progress.'

Foreign Languages

Top and middle managers are usually well educated, and most have been educated in Western universities (US, Europe, Canada, and Australia), so the English language does propagate in the world of business.

Although the English language would help you to survive in big metropoles like Shanghai, Beijing, Guangzhou, Shenzhen, or Macau, you may struggle by going a few kilometres out into the countryside.

Historically, China has over 80 languages among 56 ethnic groups, with Mandarin becoming the official language being promoted since 1956, while each city remains with their own dialect (e.g., Beijing dialect in Beijing; Shanghainese in Shanghai; and Cantonese in Hong Kong and Guangzhou).

In my experience with manufacturing partners, mainly outside of big cities, I would strongly recommend using a hired translator. There are discussions which you just cannot afford to go wrong!

Meetings

Meetings are similar to leadership: very power-centred, with teams following authority!

To create a participative atmosphere, you will need many informal talks to make people feel comfortable and safe in larger committees. There is a feeling of self-protection, which will prevent people from expressing an opinion without a second source.

'How can I please my boss?' is the main purpose! The relation comes before performance. This trend increases as you grow in seniority.

Agenda finished or not, if 1 hour is allocated for a meeting, people will stay there for an hour until they are told otherwise.

Leadership

Asia, and China in particular, have a completely different style of management from what we know in Europe.

It is crucial for the Chinese to have a model—a leader who inspires them as a patriarch—as we have known it post-WWII in Europe. They love to see leaders exercising authority, giving guidance, and sharing a vision.

Employees are of goodwill. Once they are told exactly what is expected, they will do what is asked without commenting or arguing. As in many other cultures, encouragement for self-improvement is highly appreciated and seen as a mark of interest from the supervisor.

Telling a story or a tale, ending in a moral or food for thought, is a common practice to gain staff involvement.

Time Management

Though state-owned companies and traditional enterprises punch in and out on the clock still, many industries have the implicit "996" model—9am to 9pm for 6 days a week—especially among the younger generation, who are looking for seniority in the job level.

The respect for authority drives them to respect deadlines, even if the work is incomplete or with a drop in quality.

During the Chinese New Year, usually in January or February, everything stops for 2 weeks. The second popular holiday is National Day, which is in the 1st week of October.

Organisation

The hierarchy is very clear, and there is a clear allocation of work and duties. Power is very centralised, leaving little room for delegation. The direct effect of this is that middle management is not good at decision making, and they will always 'ask the boss,' even if you decide to empower them to take responsibilities.

Chinese teams are very disciplined: They support their boss and believe that pleasing him/her is the key to success. They seldom argue and are shy to express an opinion, even if prompted.

Chapter VIII

Build a Global Supply Chain

1. Why Is It Strategic?

Competition between companies has taken very diverse forms. Globalisation has given easier access to the most efficient and cheapest technologies and production capacities, to whomever wants to embrace it. It contributes to either differentiate the level of service offered to customers, or it gives the ability to control the entire chain of operations at the lowest cost.

This is why the supply chain has taken a strategic dimension. If you intend to become a global player, serving global customers and being globally visible, you must let globalisation benefit your manufacturing process as well.

Over the last 20 years, business and personal patterns migrated from purchasing a physical product, towards purchasing a service (or a leasing). Cash being king, the trend is to invest, as capital expenditure (CapEx), only the specific equipment or tools you must have in order to produce, and subcontract the non-core activity to someone who has made it his core business.

Let's take an example of a plastic injected part. The tool costs £50k, and the press to operate it would cost £200k, plus energy, maintenance costs, additional surface in your building, and of course, the direct labour to operate it. Not to be neglected is the raw material price, accounting for around 70% of your manufacturing cost. If your volumes go up, you may struggle with capacity; if your volumes go down, your unitary cost will go up! Now let's imagine that you ask a professional moulder to do it for you. The sub-contractor has a better ability to absorb your volume variations; he most likely has a better price on raw material, since he buys in bigger volumes, and all the other attached costs (direct labour, energy, and building) are his. You have externalised the entire cost and hassle of something that is not core to your business. You spent only £50k instead of £250k, saving you £200k to be invested in something more strategic.

The most effective and profitable companies I have seen, do operate this way: being as lean as possible, externalising everything that is non-core, and keeping the high added value in house. This will require, of course, a strong team to run the entire supply chain, and that you build partnerships with suppliers, as well as have strict processes to secure quality, cost efficiency, and availability.

What?

Raw materials: You can split raw materials into 4 categories: oil and gas, metal, industrial/agricultural (textiles, rubber, or wood), and food/agricultural (coffee, cacao, sugar). All those categories are cycle sensitive and subjected to volatility. If you buy and transform any of these categories, there is a big chance that raw material will weigh between 70% and 80% of your cost of goods sold (COGS). Could purchasing be any more strategic to the profit level and long-term success of your activity?

Spare parts: Typically, these are metallic cut or plastic injected for the automotive, electrical, or electro-mechanical industry. When volume is key, you are better off asking a specialist to produce parts for you. First, there is a big chance that he can do it better than you ever would, since it is his core business. Second, you won't have the cost of capital to invest in heavy machinery that you will then be under pressure to 'feed.' And third, you will benefit from his economy of scales. Many SMEs struggle with this concept because they worry about losing their intellectual property (IP). This risk can be easily taken away by owning patents and tools that your sub-contractor will use for you. This configuration gives you the following benefits: Firstly, it is an asset in your business; secondly, it is better to pay for it upfront and have the amortisation out of your purchasing price; and thirdly, the day you want to change suppliers, you can transfer your asset to any other competitor of his.

Electronics: The market for electronic components is a truly global market, where a price is pretty similar wherever you find yourself. Mostly manufactured in Asia, the component market is controlled by a few large conglomerates. The worldwide distribution is handled by a fragmented distribution network, where Avnet and Arrow Electronics hold 30% between them.

Sub-contracting: Later in this chapter, we will review target places to relocate assembling production in which a high level of manual labour is involved. On the electronic side, a few large conglomerates operate printed circuit board (PCB) assembling plants, requiring a high level of capitalisation, and high volumes, which you may not have on your own.

Non-productive: Although purchases like land, buildings, or machine equipment (Capex) don't impact your COGS directly, they do impact your profits. All facility management costs should not be neglected, starting from logistics. In some industries, such as pipes or wood, transport can add 20%–25% to manufacturing costs, and it becomes a make or break activity.

Who?

Given the growing strategic importance of supply chains, the impulse has to come from you, the CEO. Whether your background is operations/logistics or not, you will need a solid team to run it for you. Ideally, you should have an experienced operations manager who can run your supplier's factories: Total Quality Management (TQM), Lean, Six Sigma Green/Black Belt, ERP geek. The perfect formula is to have him associated with a confirmed purchasing manager who can handle different cultures, is ready to travel, and juggles easily with currencies. Such a duo can make or break your annual income statement. So, it's important that they form a trio with their CEO. You, as a CEO, have to be the ignitor in order to support them in driving into operational excellence.

How?

Finding good suppliers is as difficult as finding good customers, with heavier consequences if you get it wrong. Trade shows, internet, mouth-to-ear, and cold calling are all sources of new potential. Identifying and qualifying them can keep your team busy full time. So I would suggest that your team focus on one particular know-how to subcontract at a time, and whilst you need to keep benchmarking your target, you move to the next activity.

The 'favourite' headache of a purchasing manager is to decide if he should double source a product by splitting the volumes (and bear a higher cost), or concentrate the volumes into one supplier for an optimised cost (and become 100% dependant on him). There isn't a good answer to this, only compromises!

So, where shall we go shopping?

2. Europe

As a direct response to the West's GATT agreement, the USSR created, in 1949, the *Council for Mutual Economic Assistance* (Comecon), in which each country behind the Iron Curtain was the centre of a specific competence, and had to follow the strict Moscow centralised planification. So, East Germany produced cars (Trabant), Poland was in the plastic industry, and Czech Republic (by then Czechoslovakia) was in machine tools and metalworking, whilst Hungary was the hub of electronics. After the fall of the wall, companies had a very steep learning curve in order to adapt to a free market economy, but quickly saw a boom of foreign direct investments. Since 2004, becoming part of the EU single market, those countries benefit from the 4 freedoms and don't have any trade barriers or tariffs. Only Slovakia is part of the Eurozone, whilst the others retained their own currency, so you must keep in mind the different exchange rates when trading with them.

Nowadays, SMEs are the main growth driver in the region, especially in Poland, Czech Republic, Slovakia, and Hungary. Part of this is because of several incentive schemes, funding opportunities, and tax reliefs. However, local SMEs keep facing challenges of excessive bureaucracy and red tape in public sector procurement. As you would, local SMEs have interests in building new bridges and partnerships with foreign companies.

Poland

Ranking 5th economy in the European single market, Poland is by far the leading country in Central Europe. The country has come a long way since its Comecon days, and is the 3rd largest global destination of outsourcing and subcontracting, just after China and India; whilst 60% of its economy is now based on service, and 30% is generated by manufacturing.

Unlike many capitals, Warsaw actually has its own strong industrial belt, called WOP (Warszawski Okręg Przemysłowy, a heritage from post-WWII), including high-tech, electrotechnical, chemical, cosmetic, construction, food processing, printing, metallurgy, machinery, and clothing. Wroclaw, in the South-West, is the second economic city. Although being firstly known for its financial services, Wroclaw is also the first choice of destination for foreign regional HQs of heavy engineering, high-tech, and pharmaceutical groups. The obvious geographical proximity with Germany and Czech Republic also makes it a first choice for logistic platforms. Nicknamed the 'European Silicon Valley,' Krakow, in the South, is a unique combination of traditional multi-nationals and a solid entrepreneur hub for start-ups. Katowice, its neighbour, transitioned successfully from a mining and heavy metallurgy city, to a modern business, conference, and trade shows centre. Gdansk, in the north, remains economically dominated by the shipbuilding industry.

Due to its strategic position, Poland became the hub for the entire region. The last 20 years have seen an ever-improving road and rail network. Whilst all the major cities have international flight connections, Warsaw might be a must-stop, depending on where you would be flying in. Seaports all along the north coast give freight and passengers easy access to the Baltic countries and Scandinavia.

Czech Republic

Historically the most technically skilled of the region, Czech Republic has retained its traditional know-how of metalworking and rotating machines. The 40% industry sector is ultra-dominated by the automotive industry: cars, buses, tramways, trucks, tractors, civil aircrafts, and even scooters. Its metalworking knowledge also extends to firearms! Manufacturing plants are spread around the country: Plzen (Pilsen), Pardubice, or Kunovice, but excluding Prague, whose 25% of the country's GDP is generated by 80% financial services. The second sector is a very diverse energy market: oil refining, natural gas, and nuclear production.

The Czech pride themselves for having the best rail network in the world. National and international access, given by a dense highway network, favours flow of goods and people, including tourists. Although a few cities do have international airports, the main hub remains Prague.

Slovakia

The historical agricultural country has completely transformed its economy over the last 20 years, becoming the first Central

European country to be accepted in the Eurozone. Encouraged by government, foreign investments are the clear driving force of the economy: low wages, low tax rates, well-educated people, stable currency, and of course, a favourable geographic location, which makes it an ideal gateway for Central Europe. Similarly to Czech Republic, the economy is dominated by services, whilst the industry sector relies heavily on the car industry. Bratislava, its capital, hosts many outsourced service divisions for world famous high-tech conglomerates. You can find some food processing, FMCG IT clusters, in the East by Nitra and Kosice.

The four main motorways connect the major national cities, as well as to Prague and Brno (CZ), and Budapest (HU) and Vienna (AT). Bratislava's airport is expanding. However, you may find it easier to land in Vienna in Austria, and take the 70km (43miles) journey on the A6 across the border.

Hungary

During the Comecon times, Hungary was the most open country to the world, with a mental closeness to the West and capitalism. As mentioned earlier, it has a strong legacy in electronics, and this keeps them positioned as the largest electronics manufacturer in Central Europe. Over the last 20 years, foreign direct investments developed and diversified the industrial landscape: food processing, pharmaceuticals, motor vehicles, information technology, chemicals, metallurgy, machinery, and electrical goods. Magyars are also very proud of the fine cuisine and undervalued wineries that boost culinary tourism. Another less known fact is that the country has been a major centre for research associated to electronics, such as mobile technologies or data security.

Following the path of its neighbours, the country's industrial sector is around 30%, whilst services jumped up to 64%. The economy is highly centralised in Budapest and its greater area.

The transport network has been highly developed over the last 20 years, and there are motorways and rail connections between all major cities. Despite having 5 official international airports, your best bet is still Budapest.

3. Asia

Asia established itself as a superpower. In the early 2000s, it was commonly believed that China was the factory of the world, whilst very few people knew that China was actually boosted by its own home market. This trend strengthened over the years: The retrocession of Hong Kong, in 1997, had opened the doors to the West for China; Singapore rose and established itself as a solid alternative to HK (which becomes even more true today); and India kept growing since the post war. The *Association of Southeast Asian Nations* (ASEAN) favours exchanges between its regional members, and during the last 20 years, albeit by ignoring the cultural differences. Japan and South Korea (the most Westernised of the region) maintained their strong foothold, whilst the Chinese state-controlled capitalism has given the world a solid alternative vs. a shaken-up Western capitalism. You can identify China developing a hegemonic position, not only economically but also militarily, with its intent to dominate the South China Sea, which can only be counterbalanced by the US military power.

China

The entrance into the World Trade Organisation (WTO), back in 2001, was the first step to becoming a world leader. China is the 2nd biggest economy in the world, since 2010, and now has a highly diversified portfolio of sectors across the economy: manufacturing, retail, mining, steel, textiles, automotive, energy generation, banking, electronics, telecommunications, e-commerce, and tourism. With megapolis around the country, and all of them having a solid mix of sectors, it is difficult to define one speciality per province. A traditional or conservative way to sub-contract in China would be to use a Hong Kong company that owns factories on the mainland. That said, it would partly cancel the cost benefit since a nice mark-up would be applied. Another option to consider is Shenzhen, just on the other side of the Hong Kong border. Back in 1978, it was the first city to be granted Special Economic Zone (SEZ) status, meaning it could open to capitalism but still live on Chinese culture. There, you will find Western-educated people, speaking proper English, and where companies are run on Western standards. However, I would strongly recommend that you employ someone locally; ideally, a shared resource with another Western company that can check the quality of your goods before shipment!

The city also offers first class freight facilities through the 'Port of Shenzhen,' the 3rd port in the world for goods, as well as for people, with its international airport. The more traditionalist people, who still prefer to fly from Hong Kong International Airport, can transfer there by ferry after having boarded and dropped their luggage on the Shenzhen side.

Taiwan

Taiwan spent years under Chinese and Japan domination, until the end of WWII. Culturally Chinese, the country benefits from an interesting combination with Japanese culture. You will commonly find joint ventures (JV), where the Japanese side brings, on the top of capital, discipline and know-how.

Since the 2000s, we have seen a continuous trend to transfer traditional labour-intensive industries into China, whilst more technology-intensive or intellectual property (IP) sensitive activities are being invested and consolidated in mainland Taiwan. Over the years, it became a high-tech hub in the region, with Western standards. Part of the recent growth is because of the increasing political instability in Hong Kong. As a result, in the same way the financial service industry transfers its activities from Hong Kong to Singapore, the sub-contracted manufacturing industry shifts towards Taiwan.

Taiwan is probably the Asian country where the economy is the most dominated by SMEs, rather than larger corporations. Their entrepreneur culture is rounded by US university or business school education. This makes them easier to approach for Western SMEs. Geographically, those companies are spread around the island and are in no way concentrated in the capital of Taipei.

South Korea

South Korea does not qualify as a low cost place where you can subcontract manufacturing or sub-assemblies. When driving through its capital, Seoul, you could easily believe you are in any major North American city, with very high costs of living.

Famous for its world-known multinationals, such as Samsung, LG, KIA, and Hyundai, the country is also rich for its SMEs and high levels of innovation. Local SMEs excel in niche products, and focus on their specific know-how. You will find them manufacturing a small range but at very high volumes for the mass markets; typically, microchips or other intelligent electronic components.

Although South Koreans establish relations on Western standards, with a good level of English, when a situation gets uncomfortable, they will quickly move back to the Asian behaviour. In one of my assignments, I was personally involved with a Seoul-based electronic component manufacturer, with whom I had a long-term and eventless relation over the years. One day, we were hit by a major quality crisis, with failure rates close to 80%. Between London and Seoul, we held daily quality crisis meetings, and the manufacturer kept telling us that 'nothing had changed on their side,' so it could only be a misuse by us or our customers. After weeks of unsuccessful email correspondence and phone calls, my purchasing manager and I boarded a plane for Seoul to solve the crisis. We were welcomed in their boardroom early in the morning, where once more we were told that the problem could not have come from their side, and that we should inquire more from our operations or customers. They agreed to have additional tests in their lab, whilst keeping us waiting alone in the room. I firmly decided not to leave until we had an answer, and we held the siege until 5pm local time, when the CEO (UK educated) eventually told us that they had transferred their production to a different factory, 6 months earlier, and had made minor changes in the processes!

This is obviously a very specific situation in a particular case; however, you should never underestimate the cultural impact, especially when tensions rise. We would have never found out the causes without having been face to face.

A review about Asia would not be complete without mentioning Malaysia or Vietnam, 2 countries that are part of the ASEAN Free Trade Association. Malaysia had a strong expansion over the last 15 years, and can be less and less considered as a low cost country. If you can still find former foreign direct investments (FDI) (mostly from USA) that manufacture locally, and export back to North America, it is not the case of new investments anymore. Vietnam, whilst being behind Malaysia in term of development, is a favourite place for FDIs. Here again, it is driven by its own market, and many investors use Vietnam as a regional base to shine across the ASEAN region.

4. Americas

Whilst we all live in a global world, it can be difficult to argue with geography. This section hints to local sourcing options to serve local or regional markets. We will consider Mexico as a base for North America, and Brazil as a base for South America. I have rarely seen finished or semi-finished goods sub-contracted in Brazil for being re-exported into Europe.

Mexico

Mexico can be an ideal gateway to access American markets for non-American direct investors. It still is a low cost country, albeit with very high disparity, where locally manufactured or sub-assembled goods have access into the US-Mexico-Canada agreement (USMCA). Mexico is famously known for being the biggest car producer for the entire continent. US automotive conglomerates started to implant factories in the 30s, whilst Asian and European manufacturers arrived only in the 60s. Less known is the dominance of electronics, which has grown exponentially since 2010: televisions, mobile phones, electronic appliances for finished goods or printed circuits boards, and semiconductors for semi-finished goods. Mexico is the world's 6th largest electronic manufacturer, behind China, USA, Japan, South Korea, and Taiwan. Mexico's 30% of exports are electronics, and 70% have North America as the destination.

You have not forgotten that the M in MINT stands for Mexico (see Chapter II), and as such is considered as one of the potentially biggest growing countries, firstly boosted by its own market. So we can expect a sustainable growth in manufacturing costs, as much as in cost of living.

Brazil

Brazil is the biggest country in South America and is the B in BRIC (see Chapter II). Its size and its own growth rate makes it an attractive market in itself. On top of its natural resources, the economy is very diverse: energy, automotive, electro-technical, steel, and food processing.

A direct investment in Brazil not only gives you a spot in a large, growing market, but it also opens the door to the rest of South America, through the Mercosur alliance.

An additional incentive is the contribution of SMEs that generate 30% of the GDP. This should help you to find local partners to help your presence in the region. I would strongly recommend you find people who speak Portuguese and can understand local cultures, before starting any venture in the area.

5. Africa

North Africa is to France what Mexico is to North America: an ideal location for sub-assembling partnerships. Morocco and Tunisia are pleasant countries, situated in the continental Europe time zone, a 3-hour flight from Paris, and where French is widely spoken. Probably inherited from the textile sub-contracting times, both countries have a know-how and ability in plastic injection, electro mechanical assembling, and electronic soldering. Politically, both countries are stable.

Like Mexico for North America, non-European companies could use those 2 countries as a sub-assembling base to enter Europe; France, in particular.

Should your volumes not be enough to justify a direct investment, the safest option would be to find a local sub-contractor. If you are not comfortable enough to venture directly with a local company, I would recommend you search some French companies specialised in your area: they most likely have either a partner or an owned operation. They would be happy to support you, but you would lose a part of your cost savings.

Chapter IX

Generate Global Sales

1. Internal and External Sales Teams

A common mistake made by many organisations is to consider the external sales people as the hunters, and the internal sales team as the *'back office'* or *'customer support team.'* I found it very effective to rename it *'Internal Sales Team'*: more than only a renaming, you need to drive the cultural change. An internal sales team talks or communicates to an average of 300 people per day (from which 50 are by phone, and 250 are by mail), whilst a driven external sales force makes an average of 6 to 8 visits per day, plus a few phone calls between meetings. This means that your internal sales team can cover far much ground and still make sure the *customer experience* is up to the mark. In *customer experience*, you need to include availability, on-time delivery—and not to forget a too-often-taken-for-granted technical support—pre sales or after sales! An internal sales team is better able to nurture the everyday relation with customers than externals are, and should be recognised and remunerated as such. You may want to make sure you reward them in an appropriate and motivating way!

It's absolutely crucial that your internal and external teams work hand in hand as equals and not in parallel silos; or even worse, as internal assistants to external superiors. I have an anecdote where a long-time servant head of the internal sales team called a senior regional sales manager, who had been working for the company for over 18 months:

'Hi Jack! It's Jo!'
'Jo who?'
'Jo from the office!'
'Do we know each other? Have we met before?'

This silly example (but sadly true) demonstrates how much of a gap can be created between an internal and external team! Think about how much energy, coordinated teamwork, and per-formance can be generated daily on a healthy basis! ONE TEAM! It will take time and management to change attitude and cul-ture, but once you succeed, it will be a powerful team. I do re-member once, when on the 30th of the month, a rather young junior member of the internal team called up a senior external member: "You have until tomorrow to find another £12,500 to make budget this month. Where can we find it?" Isn't this pow-erful?

2. OEM Accounts

An *Original Equipment Manufacturer* (OEM) account has many different definitions, depending on which industry you find your-self in. The literal way to read it is that you are the original equip-ment manufacturer for someone else. In this section, we would consider it as a customer who integrates your products, either finished or semi-finished in his range, by replacing your brand with his. One of the first benefits of such accounts is that they generate volumes.

Although you would sell to a lower margin, you will see large volumes of identical products going through your factory, helping you to cover your fixed costs, and amortising your tools faster. You can almost immediately improve your direct margin to such accounts; most of the time, they order by large batches and do not need individual packaging like you may use for your other types of customers. Production planning teams and your suppliers do like OEM accounts, since they can work on monthly forecasts a year in advance and are able to smooth down supply chain peaks.

The advantage for your customer is to complete his range whilst benefiting from your economies of scales. An OEM can buy proven working items without having to invest in its own developments, component sourcing, or manufacturing capital investment equipment. An OEM partnership is for the long term: Your product specifications in their documentations (catalogues or Bill of Material) are hard and very costly to remove, and this makes it very difficult for your competition to replace you. It is also an easy and cost effective way to expand your reach: If he goes global, he will take you with him. The archetype is in the automotive industry: Suppliers follow their final car manufacturers all over the globe.

Another dimension to keep in mind is that you actually don't control an OEM; you just follow him. If he does well, you do well. If his volumes come down, yours come down too!

A good OEM account should be a larger organisation than yours—ideally a multinational. Your product(s) shall be sold all over the globe, giving you access to markets out of your reach, and giving a larger exposure than you would ever have. Their process and standards will give you reliable forecasts, and although the involved volumes are not core business and are probably little volumes for them, they will make a nice contribution to yours. You will struggle to find such advantages coming from a smaller organisation than you are.

This is a common practice between companies from different sizes, to private label for a competitor or a manufacturer in a parallel industry. Your product will bear a different brand and logo. Although such agreements are made under different forms of confidentiality agreements, the industry does recognise the origin of items by their design or function. This can potentially **upgrade** your **brand**.

You and your board must be the guardians of this practice in order to avoid dangers and value-destructive drifts. Such agreements should be dedicated for manufacturers only (the clue is in the name), and with guaranteed volumes. So it is your decision to set the minimum volumes you would be happy with to enter into such a contractual agreement. You may find a minimum of 1% of your total revenue threshold being a good marker. A trap that is very easy to fall into is to start labelling for everyone who is not a manufacturer, and with no minimum quantities; you will end up labelling for one piece per year, for the local plumber (and eventually chase payment). This will definitely **downgrade** your **brand**.

OEM = High Volumes + Low Margin + Long Term + (potential) Brand Upgrade + Globalisation by following

3. Distribution

One of my success stories with distribution was to double sales in 1 year, and multiply by 5, over 5 years!

I do have a particular affinity for distribution. When well set and organised, it can be a powerful channel partner and become your winning horse for a long race. We can compare distribution to a massive sea liner: heavy to move, long to get started, but once set and launched, it ploughs through, goes far, and won't stop unless you really want it to and put an iceberg in its way.

You will find a very wide range of distributors: from representation offices of 1 person for a small region, to larger multinationals, such as Point P (Saint Gobain group), B&Q DIY giant (Kingfisher group), or Rexel in the specialised wholesale. A large distributor can generate a worldwide coverage for you, and promote your brand in countries you would never address directly.

Amongst the benefits of a distributor, you will find a large sales force that you could never afford on your own, which will open new doors for you. A distributor will expand your market coverage by relaying your *brand* through more outlets and representations with delocalised inventories across the covered territory. The ultimate bonus is that, if incentivised properly, such a channel partner will phase your competition out by cross selling them to your products. From a financial perspective, he will serve smaller accounts in a much more cost efficient way than you ever could, and even take the financial payment risk!

In contrast, you ought to be careful of not putting all your eggs in the same basket, and by making sure you have several different distributors. Mechanically, as volumes do grow, your distributors will have a heavier bargaining power over you, and you need to be ready to face your annual rounds of negotiation. Something you never go around with distribution are rebate schemes: You do have to be in full control of the implication of the mechanism; or by the end of the year, you will wake up with a terrible headache. Your biggest asset to control your distribution is your **brand**. If your brand is strong enough, distribution cannot afford to not have you on their shelves. As seen in a previous chapter, your **brand** is your biggest asset!

In one of my latest appointments, I was fortunate enough to bind a personal relationship with the COO of the biggest distributor in my home market, and after years of rivalry and suspicion, our newly built relation became the success story of each other's organisation. We first started by establishing the '10 command-ments,' under which both sales organisations would obey. This was first perceived with irony and sarcasm since such commitment never lasted over a month. The COO and I agreed to keep a direct phone line to each other and report any arising issues, and address them before they would make waves. Surprisingly, people started to trust each other, to share information, and to work with each other as ONE team.

Distribution = Sales costs are variable + reduced margin + short to mid-term + brand exposure + globalisation by following

4. Installers

By definition, this customer segment installs and commissions your product, as would a plumber, an electrician, or a kitchen installer.

This is the heart and the core base of your business: people who use your product and who are, most of the time, final decision makers. From wherever the installer chooses to buy your products from, he should always have direct contact with you so that he can enjoy the value of your ***brand***. It can be for basic technical questions, help in selecting his products, feeding market information back to you, and projects he works on, or simply having the feeling he belongs to your ***brand***.

Your relation with this segment permits you to keep a pulse on the market and its trends. Who better than people using your products to tell you which additional functions it should have, what makes their lives easier, or what is expected from the end users, his customer, and your final customer in the chain?

Too often, manufacturers find themselves competing with their own distributors, and rivalry may arise about whose customer it actually is! With a strong distribution policy, such issues do not happen. The idea is to split the information flows from the goods flows. Why could an installer not have the information flow with manufacturers, whilst he prefers to have the goods flow with your distributor? What prevents you and the distributor from organising common customer visits? The combination of your two organisations must increase the offered value. Why could you, as a manufacturer, not offer first class training or motivating seminars? Such seminars can even be organised at the distributors premises, who would obviously be more local that you would!

You will find training sessions and seminars very useful in many senses:

- First, you actually do train your customers on your products; if they are trained on yours, they may not use your competitor's!
- Second, you build triparty relations between your teams, distribution, and installers, which generates a dynamic—a ONE TEAM feeling! This will pay back short, medium, and long term.
- Three, you give everyone an experience to enjoy and remember.

Once you have reached a certain recurring volume of trainees, you may even choose to create your own training centre or academy!

In whatever industry you look, one of the specificity of the installer segment is his high level of fragmentation. Five per cent of the companies are large or very large, whilst 95% are under 5 people; so as the Brits say: The market has a very long tail.

Nowadays, there are many ways to touch such a fragmented population, but a SME will find it difficult to serve all the market directly; hence, the added value of distribution supporting your sales effort on a fair share of it. Eventually, your ultimate goal is to have installers faithful to your **brand**, wherever they decide to buy it from.

Installer = Higher margin + higher cost to serve + very short term + maximum brand exposure

5. Specifiers

Those are the people who recommend your offer without having any physical involvement with it. The most common example of a specifier is a doctor, who prescribes you some particular medicine because he believes this is what you need and will fix your problem. More largely, we could refer to architects in everything related to the construction and building industry, from concrete to kitchen appliances, via your heating system or lighting appliances. Another example could be professors in their field of expertise, recommending particular capital equipment goods in industries such as plastics, geology, or aeronautics. Once a specifier is convinced of your offering answering a specific problem, he will specify and recommend your brand and part number in his specifications file. This is how you control your downstream actors: installers, and certainly not distributors, will recommend a product against an established professional who is an authority in the market.

The purpose of this section is to highlight this forgotten segment. Why, if so effective, don't we see more commercial actions towards specifiers? Companies, and especially SME, rarely allocate resources and efforts towards specifiers, since the benefits are medium to long term. It demands a particular type of sales person to address them: technically aware, and hungry to demonstrate products without having the benefit of a sale! You may find sales people enjoying the talk without being measured, but CEOs don't!

There is a safe and cost effective way to act on a specifier for SME. Most of SME have an important yearly cost to bear: catalogues. Everyone who has been involved with a printing agency knows how volume sensitive the industry is. As an example, you may find that the total cost for 6,000 catalogues is the same as for 10,000 catalogues. So, since a rerun would cost a fortune, SME go for 10,000 copies... and at the end of the year are left with 1,000. With most catalogues being dated and modified for the following year, your current stock becomes obsolete. Instead of binning them, why don't you gift them to people who may have the use of your offer one day, or who could recommend them to others?

In the diverse companies I have worked for, we granted the obsolete catalogues to schools dedicated to our industry. First students love to use real material for their studies; they learn to know your brand, and learn your offering and part numbers. Once they become active professionally, guess which brand, which manufacturer, and which part numbers will come straight to their minds?

Actions towards specifiers have to be made locally since, most of the time, you will be talking to individuals. A situation in which you could find yourself acting more globally, is (once more) talking to a multinational headquartered in one country, and deciding what should be done in other countries or the other way around: your specification work in one country generates fruits in others.

Specifier = Long term + no measure of efficiency + brand promotion in intellectual circles

Chapter X

Maximise Your Value and Prepare to Cash In

X

The best exit strategy is the one that best fits your company and your personal goals. Decide first what you want to walk away with. If it's just money, an exit strategy, such as selling on the open market or to another business, may be the best pick. If you are more concerned with the legacy you want to leave behind you, then family succession or selling to your employees might be best for you.

Whichever exit strategy you choose, you need to start working on it. Planning in advance gives you the time to do it right, and to maximise your returns.

1. KPIs and Value Drivers

The key performance indicators (KPIs) you have set in the Strategy Review Process™ must be religion for you, as well as for the entire organisation. You will find a full battery of performance, profitability, efficiency ratios, or more, on the Return on Equity levers. However, I recommend to focus only on a few to keep it simple. Make sure everyone in your organisation understands these basics indicators and learns to drive with numbers.

• Revenue
• GM & GM%: Gross Margin

- EBIT: Earnings Before Interest and Taxes. This is your *operating profit.*
- EBITDA: Which is EBIT + Depreciation + Amortization. This is how much *cash* you generate.
- Cash level: Your bank accounts
- Working Capital Funding Gap: Inventory + Receivables - Payables
- Value Creation = Return on Capital Employed (ROCE) – Weighted Average Cost of Capital (WACC)

Those KPIs guide you to drive your value up and help you and potential buyers to calculate a first enterprise value. This is the first level on which you build up your value. Therefore, you need to demonstrate solid intangible assets, called *Goodwills.*

Financial Transparency

Demonstrate how well the company is driven with numbers, with your monthly management accounts, KPIs follow-up, cash management (debts and receivables), and cash flow monitoring. Those basic elements will build confidence in the analysed numbers and how the company is managed.

Executive Team

Too many SMEs are far too dependent on their owners. A potential buyer will be worried about how much value the company will lose once he buys you out. If you suffer from the 'superhero complex' and can't let go of the decision making process, be ready for a proper value cut.

The opposite solution is to have a proper executive team that owner(s) can trust and delegate. Empower, lead, train, and let them fail. Your payback is exponential.

Every time I was involved in a company where the executive team had shares in the business, the company overperformed. When every decision maker has a stake in the company value, you as a CEO have little need to carry out some cost cutting plans, or worry about who flies business class or economy! Your team will sort it out between themselves without you even knowing about it.

Level of Internationalisation

How global are you? How do you split your revenue, gross margin, and profit across countries? How much do you purchase or subcontract abroad? Imagine you have a fully operative organisation in one of the single market areas we have seen in Chapter V. How much value would this have? How many different nationalities do you have in your teams? How many languages are spoken in your organisation?

In my latest role, I led a UK based manufacturing SME, whose 35% of its revenue was coming from continental Europe. The loss of access to the single market pushed us to set up a European entity with its own logistic platform in order to retain the full benefits and ensure frictionless trading with our continental customer base. This legal entity, employees, and customers represent a 'Goodwill' value; especially for any non-European potential buyer who wants to retain access to a 300M people market.

Brand

The value of your brand is a direct value to your enterprise. A buyer will buy everything your brand stands for (see Chapter IV): your values, your culture, your people, your market access, international customer database, websites, and social media traffic. Part of the brand value is also how much more money your customers are paying compared to a similar product made by your competitors.

2. Keep Your Costs Under Control

A P&L is composed of 3 triggers: revenue, gross margin, and fixed costs. In whatever industry sector you find yourself, only one of them is a certitude: fixed costs. With little control over revenue or gross margin, you are left with controlling your cost structure; and the more rigorously, the more you can shape your profit and enterprise value.

Manufacturing

One of the secrets is to be as lean and resilient as possible: Keep a maximum of cost variable. The more your costs are variable, the less you will be submitted to revenue fluctuation, or be at the mercy of a raw material shortage.

Do you actually need your own heavy machines? Your injection press? Your own extrusion line? Your own metal forming workshop with surface treatment and painting installation? Do you actually have the necessary volumes to 'feed' such capital-intensive equipment?

By subcontracting, you firstly ask a specialist, for whom it is their bread and butter, to do a job which is not your core business. Second, although you will pay a mark-up, you will still benefit from his economy of scales. In Chapter VIII, you saw where to find the best and most cost effective experts in your needed field.

Having your own machine increases your capital expenditures and decreases your ROCE! By subcontracting, your transform your fixed cost into a variable cost, and keep your cash in your own bank account. This also has its benefits from a management perspective. Imagine some of your competitors get nervous and trigger market price reductions. Psychologically, you will be tempted to follow the trend just for the purpose of keeping your machines running. When, by a subcontractor, your procurement team will just reduce the replenishment planning! When the opposite happens, and your sales team brings you elephant-sized orders, a specialist will be in a better place to absorb the volume increase and to juggle with its capacity.

	Cash	Revenue	Variable Cost	Fixed Cost	ROCE
Own machines	↓	→	→	↑	↓
Subcontract	→	→	↑	→	→

Here again, this can become a philosophical discussion like we had in Chapter I. Is your model built on a patrimonial culture (Mittelstand), or do you look at it as an asset (Brittelstand)?

Monkeys on the Table

Do you remember the story of the 'monkey on the table,' from Chapter VI? I have news for you: If you haven't dealt with the situation, the monkeys will still be there! Whilst you have accepted, year after year, a profit hit, you now will face a final bill. Indeed, since their costs directly impact your EBITDA line, it also impacts your company valuation, and these costs now are multiplied by your agreed multiple. Just imagine, your acquirer offers you a multiple of 8, and your monkey(s) cost you a total of £100,000 per annum: You are looking at £800,000 knocked off your sales price. Loyalty might be priceless, but at least you know its cost.

IT

You may consider IT and ERP systems a bore or a necessary evil. I do tend to agree with you, and so do CEOs I am talking to. However, if implemented correctly and used appropriately, you can turn it into a very powerful tool to keep your teams focused, and drive through clearly identified and communicated indicators. I would also recommend you upgrade or at least update your systems regularly, or you will soon have in hand an inoperative, outdated system. If you ignore it and take it for granted, it will catch up with you in a very painful way: operatively and financially. It is worth the investment.

One of the additional benefits of a proper IT system is electronic invoicing. Have you ever calculated how much an invoice costs you: paper; printing; paying someone to fold it, put it in an envelope, and stamp it; and franking machine rental? I recommend you to do the exercise. Take the result and apply your multiplier—you are in for a surprise. It will cover for a few ERP updates.

3. When? Your 'Strategic Exit Window'

As many other things in life, you have times when acquisitions happen everywhere, and others when it is quiet for a while. Acquisitions have their cycles too. A good time to sell is when you can see all the signs of a consolidating industry:

- Revenue growth slows down.
- Margins start reducing.
- Your product becomes a commodity.
- The market becomes a race for volumes and low prices.

This is when you start seeing other actors acquiring each other. The pace of acquisitions is directly linked to the competitive intensity and how fast market prices and margins drop. The faster the acquisitions happen, the more nervous the industry becomes, and the higher your price tag becomes. Your big risk is to be the last one left behind when all other players have gained twice or three times your size. This is what I call the *Strategic Exit Window*. If you hold on for too long and miss the window, your price tag falls off a cliff. Why would someone still buy once it became easier and cheaper to buy your market shares and destroy you commercially?

In the different diligence processes I have conducted over the years, and the consolidating industries I have been active in, I have never seen a SME sold too early, but almost always too late. SME owners hold on for far too long. Emotionally attached, the value of their 'baby' is worth much more to them than what numbers can possibly demonstrate, or what any potential buyer would pay. I have seen an owner receiving a flattering first offer, but decided to wait, wait, and wait. Emotionally, the majority of owners were not ready. Sadly, when they were ready to let it go, the value had sharply fallen, and they sold for a third of the value of the original offer, at the despair of the minor shareholders. I have this other example of a declining industry company I worked for: The family attached a price tag of €40 Mio, whilst it had been making losses for the last 4 years. This is another sure way to never sell your baby: Put a price tag that nobody will pay.

4. How Much? Value Your Company

If your SME is stock listed, the value is given by your floating share price. In the case of a takeover bid (friendly or aggressive), the buyer might offer a premium to incentivise shareholders to give away their share of control. In the case of non-listed companies, the two most commonly used valuation methods are multiples and discounted cash flows.

Multiples

In the past, we used multiple of EBIT, when a company value was based on its capacity to generate profits. Over the last decade, we have seen a shift towards EBITDA, which demonstrates that the capacity of generating cash has now taken over profit generation. This indicator is simply multiplied by an agreed coefficient.

This so-called multiple will be determined through analysing the past performance of your business, as well as benchmarking other companies with similar activity, such as your competitors or industry peers. Your auditors or sector broker specialists can help you to identify the range of this multiplier.

As an example, in the last few years, the average multiplier for UK SMEs transactions has been in the range of 3 to 6. If the enterprise has owners not involved in the daily business, the average goes up to 6 to 8. In the case of a single-person business, the multiplier is below 0.5: Indeed, once the person is bought out, the company is left with some equipment and a customer database.

For a SME, I would recommend a very easy and conservative way to evaluate your business. In Fig 10.1, a simple yearly update of this chart will give you an accurate value of what your asset is worth.

Share Value Calculation

Year	EBITDA £000		Multiple	EBITDA £000	
2018	£	1,500	1x	£	1,500
2019	£	2,000	2x	£	4,000
2020	£	2,500	3x	£	7,500
Total				£	13,000
Weighted Average EBITDA				£	2,167
Industry EBITDA multiple				5	
Value				£	10,833
Surplus Cash 31/12/2020				£	2,000
Company Valuation				**£**	**12,833**
Issued number of shares				100,000	
Price per share				**£**	**128.33**

A few years ago, a privately invested company from my sector, which we shall call XYZ, was sold to a Nasdaq listed multinational for an astronomical 22x EBITDA and 8x revenue, whilst our industry EBITDA multiplier oscillated between 8 and 10. Someone had obviously been doing a good sell job to a person who hasn't been doing too good a purchasing job. I do remember that this acquisition did not impress their shareholders, and it contributed to a sharp fall of its share price. So, how could this happen?

Discounted Cash Flows (DCF)

This method looks into the future and relies on assumptions of future incomes. DCF estimates what future cash flow would be worth today, so you apply a discount to integrate the risk and time value of the money. The idea is that £1 is worth more today than tomorrow. To work out the present value of future cash flows, you discount them by the post-acquisition WACC.

The core concept of this method is that you sell growth that you haven't yet generated. In order to increase your company value, this method will tempt you to overpromise and announce very ambitious future growth. I was once, as a potential acquirer, doing due diligence work for a company that promised 15% growth per annum over the next 5 years, whilst they hadn't even delivered 5% per annum over the last 3 years. Overpromising is very tempting, and this is why every memorandum has a sales forecast in the form of a hockey stick. In the case of XYZ, it obviously worked out in the favour of the seller.

5. To Whom? Identify Your Potential Buyers

The most common method to sell your company is like selling a property: You appoint a broker. You will also find that auditors and bankers can also play the role of go-between in such transactions; they talk every day to entrepreneurs like you.

Strategic Buyer

The archetype of a strategic buyer is a competitor. He wants your market shares, access to markets, your product ranges, consolidated operations, and of course, to get rid of a competitor. Common but very sensitive too: If the deal does not go through, your competitor will have a deep understanding of your organisation, strengths, and weaknesses. Although they will have signed a non-disclosure agreement (NDA), they cannot 'unsee' what they have seen, nor forget what they learnt about you.

But you may also find your buyer in your existing supply chain. One of your suppliers could have an interest in your sales channels and acquire you for your sales and marketing expertise. This is called: *Downstream Value absorption.*

On the other side of the supply chain are customers. If you are an important enough supplier to them, they may want to gain control over you and own your know-how. This is called: *Upstream Value absorption.*

Strategic buyers are the category from which you may get the best offer, since they are the ones most likely to make financial gains on future synergies.

Financial Investor

Better known under the name private equity (PE), they are financed by pension funds, insurance companies, or wealthy direct individual investors. A PE house is after 2 things:

- Cash generation to pay out dividends to their investors, and finance further acquisitions
- Potential financial return by a high multiplier, through a resell within the next 3 to 5 years

Since the key success driver for a PE house is the return factor, they are much more aggressive on the acquisition price. However, PE is a good fit if your company needs more cash, as they will support further investments.

Individual Investor

Depending on the size and value of your company, an individual or a group of individuals may buy you out. This category is called *venture capitalist* (VC). Typically, it could be individuals in their mid-career, who have left a senior position in a multinational and are attracted by an entrepreneurial adventure.

Employees

A management buyout (MBO) is a mechanism that could seduce you if you stand more on the legacy side. Your executive team is the best and safest option to ensure business continuity for any stakeholders. Selling to them won't cost you any broking fees or due diligence work.

However, you have to be ready to take a serious cut: Your management team will not likely be in a position to pay you the sort of premium a strategic buyer would.

IPO

The most ambitious way to sell your business is to float it through an initial public offering (IPO). You basically sell your shares to the general public, entitling them to dividends and ultimately company control. Although very tempting, an IPO has a high cost since it involves insurance companies and legal firms, and you will need to hire some 'financial marketing' know-how. You are not selling products or services anymore, but your enterprise value. An IPO is also a sword with two edges: The market decides the value of your company, for the best or for the worst.

6. How? Prepare for Your Due Diligence Process

It can be very daunting when you appoint a broker and kick off a sales process, so I would recommend that you and your teams—particularly your company secretary—start building up a library of documents that you will be requested to provide during any exit process.

You will find, hereafter, a non-exhaustive list of the first items, and you can find a more comprehensive checklist on my website.

Management

- Last 3 years of minutes of board meetings
- Strategy Document™
- KPI dashboards

Commercial

- Client data analysis
- Carer data analysis
- Local competitive analysis
- Local demographics

HR

- Org chart of company structure
- Identify any future gaps in staffing
- Contracts of employment
- Job descriptions

Operational

- Operations manual
- ISO certifications

IT

- Review of current systems
- Updated certificates
- Data compliance

Financial

- Management accounts
- Last 3 years of full accounts (income, balance sheet, and cash flow statements)
- Tax statements
- Bank statements

Legal

- Building lease
- Job descriptions
- Contracts of employment

ABOUT THE AUTHOR

French-German by blood and born in Strasbourg, Sandy Damm could easily be described as a 'global citizen.' His 20+ years of professional activity have taken him all around the globe, during which time he has lived in France, Germany, Switzerland, USA and United Arabic Emirates. Since 2014, he has been based in the United Kingdom, where until recently he ran Sontay Ltd., a privately invested, leading manufacturer of sensors for the building controls industry. After having multiplied the share value by 3.5, he successfully exited in November 2020, leaving behind him a well performing team on a solid financial, market and product basis.

Whether as Managing Director, CEO or Divisional Managing Director, Sandy has held P&L responsibilities ranging from £5m to £90m revenue on behalf of privately invested, family-owned and multinational firms. Driven by results and achievements, he has built and managed teams in Europe, Middle East, North America and Asia-Pacific. He has been involved in turnarounds as well as mergers & acquisitions on both the buying and the selling side.

Currently in transition, Sandy conducts due diligence processes for various private equity funds firms looking to enlarge their manufacturing SME portfolios. As an author and consultant, he offers businesses and organisations the tools to create a successful transformation through the internationalisation process, and strategies to meet goals and long-term objectives.

Sandy graduated from Harvard Business School's GMP (General Management Program) in 2020, and has held an Executive MBA from EMLyon since 2005. He also holds various certifications in geopolitics and financial valuation.

Printed in Great Britain
by Amazon